T5-CVE-299

INNOVATIVE MINDS

JACQUES-YVES COUSTEAU

EXPLORING THE WONDERS OF THE DEEP

Lois Markham

RSVP

**RAINTREE
STECK-VAUGHN**
PUBLISHERS
The Steck-Vaughn Company

Austin, Texas

To Stephen

Published by Raintree Steck-Vaughn Publishers, an imprint of Steck-Vaughn Company.

Series created by Blackbirch Graphics
Series Editor: Tanya Lee Stone
Editor: Lisa Clyde Nielsen
Associate Editor: Elizabeth M. Taylor
Production/Design Editor: Calico Harington

Raintree Steck-Vaughn Publishing Staff
Editors: Shirley Shalit, Kathy DeVico
Project Manager: Lyda Guz

Library of Congress Cataloging-in-Publication Data

Markham, Lois.
    Jacques-Yves Cousteau: exploring the wonders of the deep / by Lois Markham.
        p.   cm. — (Innovative minds)
    Includes bibliographical references (p.   ) and index.
    Summary: Surveys the life and accomplishments of the celebrated French oceanographer.
    ISBN 0-8172-4404-2
    1. Cousteau, Jacques-Yves—Juvenile literature. 2. Oceanographers—France—Biography—Juvenile literature. [1. Cousteau, Jacques-Yves.]   I. Title. II. Series.
GC30.C6M373   1997
551'.46'0092—dc20
[B]   96-19497
                                                                                    CIP
                                                                                     AC

Printed in the United States of America
1 2 3 4 5 6 7 8 9 0   LB   00 99 98 97 96

TABLE OF CONTENTS

Jacques Cousteau invented many new devices to improve deep-sea diving, but perhaps his biggest contribution was bringing the undersea world to millions of people—via their television sets.

A Boyhood
On the
Move

One morning in January 1943, a tall, thin man, wearing just a bathing suit and carrying two heavy tanks of compressed air on his back, waded into the frigid waters of the Marne River outside Paris, France. A diving mask covered his eyes and nose. Twin hoses dangled from a rubber mouthpiece, connecting it to the air tanks.

While his companions shivered on the bank of the river, Jacques-Yves Cousteau fitted the mouthpiece between his lips. Then, he slowly sank into the water. Soon he was completely submerged. Nothing—no breathing tubes or guide ropes—connected him to the surface. Bubbles rising to the surface, however, revealed that he was breathing underwater.

Suddenly, the bubbles stopped. Those on the shore held their breath. A few minutes passed. Finally, Émile Gagnan, one of the observers, could bear the suspense no longer. He threw off his coat and began to untie his shoelaces: He would brave the icy waters to rescue his friend. But wait! Cousteau was surfacing. Wading back to his companions, he complained that the underwater breathing device that he and Gagnan had created did not work as they had hoped. Even though it was an improvement over earlier such devices, it was not perfect, and anything less than perfection was not good enough for Jacques Cousteau.

Silently, Cousteau and Gagnan got in the car for the drive back to Paris. For a short time, they were deep in thought. Almost at the same instant, both realized the mistake that they had made in the design of the breathing device. Exploding into rapid-fire dialogue, they reviewed the problem and came up with a solution: A simple change would remedy the problems, they were sure. They would call their invention the aqualung. With growing excitement, they realized that success—and with it a revolution in underwater exploration—was within their grasp.

THE EARLY YEARS

Who was this man who was about to revolutionize underwater diving? Where had he come from?

Jacques-Yves Cousteau was the second of two sons of Daniel and Elizabeth Cousteau. Daniel and Elizabeth came from prominent families in Saint-André-de-Cubzac, a market town in the Bordeaux wine-producing region of France, about a day's train ride south of Paris. Daniel was one of four sons of a notary who functioned as a lawyer, executor of deeds, real estate sales, and marriage contracts. Daniel was the only son who was sent to law school and could have inherited his father's practice had he not preferred to broaden his horizons. Elizabeth came from the wealthiest family in town.

When they married, he was 31, and she was 18. In 1906, they left the sleepy little town, right after their marriage. Daniel in particular was looking for a more adventurous life than Saint-André-de-Cubzac could provide. He found it in Paris, working as a legal advisor and companion to a wealthy American named James Hazen. Hazen was the 31-year-old son of the founder of the Equitable Life Assurance Society.

The Cousteaus remained in Paris for the birth of their first son, Pierre-Antoine, in 1906. A few years later, however, when Elizabeth was expecting their second child, the family traveled back to Saint-André-de-Cubzac. They wanted to be in the ancestral home, Elizabeth's family's country home, on the banks of the Dordogne River, for the birth. It was there that Jacques was born, on June 11, 1910. A beautiful child, he was plump and smiling, with a full head of black hair.

After the rest of the family had a chance to admire young Jacques, his parents took him and Pierre back to Paris. It was the first of many trips that Jacques would make during his boyhood. Daniel's employer traveled around Europe a great deal, and he insisted that his advisor accompany him. When Pierre and Jacques were young, the whole family traveled with Daniel. Jacques Cousteau's earliest memory is of being lulled to sleep by the rocking motion of a train.

Cousteau also remembers being fascinated with water since the age of four or five. He especially loved the physical sensation of touching it. He also loved thinking about it. Sitting on the shore, Jacques watched large ships pass by and often wondered why they did not sink. This led to more questions. Why did human beings float for example, and stones did not?

Jacques had much time to ponder these questions. For the first seven years of his life, he suffered from chronic enteritis, an inflammation of the intestines. The family doctor discouraged the boy from engaging in strenuous exercise. So Jacques had time to think—and read. His favorite books were adventure stories of the sea, tales of daring pirates, smugglers, and Red Sea pearl divers. Through books, he experienced the adventures that his frail body would not permit him to have.

As a result of Jacques's intestinal problems, the chubby baby had become an extremely thin child. It was the shape that his body would have for the rest of his life.

In 1914, when Jacques was four years old, World War I broke out in Europe. France was a primary battleground. Although German troops never reached Paris, the city was not the gay, exciting place that it had been before the war. Daniel Cousteau and his employer quarreled, and Daniel soon found himself without a job. With Daniel unemployed and two young children to care for, the Cousteaus had to rely on money from Elizabeth's family.

In 1918, the war finally ended. Once again, wealthy Americans flocked to Paris to enjoy its charms. Daniel found another position as companion and legal advisor to one of them. Eugene Higgins, a bachelor in his sixties, owned lavish homes in New York City, New Jersey, and Paris. He also kept a large yacht in Deauville, France—a town on the English Channel—for summer cruises.

Young Jacques loved to read adventure books, such as
Jules Verne's *Twenty Thousand Leagues Under the
Sea,* in which a giant octopus attacked a submarine.

Like Daniel's former employer, Higgins expected his advisor to travel with him. Now, however, Pierre and Jacques were old enough to be in school. So while Daniel and Elizabeth toured with Higgins, their sons spent most of the year at boarding school. Observing from a distance the exciting life his parents led made Jacques long to be a world traveler.

Higgins was a strong believer in physical fitness. When he saw Jacques, who had gotten anemia after recovering from enteritis, he urged the Cousteaus to ignore the doctor's warning against strenuous exercise. Jacques, he said, should learn to swim. And so Jacques did learn to swim and, thanks to Higgins, discovered yet another way to continue his love affair with water.

The Young Explorer

In 1920, when Jacques was ten years old, Eugene Higgins decided to return to his New York City home for an extended stay. He insisted that the entire Cousteau family come with him. After traveling by ship across the Atlantic Ocean, the Cousteaus settled into an apartment on West 95th Street in New York City. Jacques attended Holy Name School, and Pierre was enrolled in a public high school. The boys quickly became fluent in English. For a while, Jacques even took to calling himself Jack.

After school and on weekends, neighborhood friends taught Pierre and Jacques to play stickball in the street. In return, the two French boys created a sensation by introducing their New York friends to European two-wheeled roller skates. Jacques admired his older brother and willingly followed Pierre in such daring escapades as dangling from apartment fire escapes.

While in the United States, Jacques and Pierre attended a summer camp on Lake Harvey in Vermont. Camp brought both good and bad experiences for Jacques. One of the camp instructors, Mr. Boetz, insisted that Jacques try horseback riding. Even after young Jacques had fallen off a horse several times, Mr. Boetz kept him at it. Much later in life, Cousteau wrote about the experience, concluding that he still hated horses.

The stern Mr. Boetz was also part of Jacques's first diving experiences. There are at least two versions of the story. According to one, Mr. Boetz required Jacques, as punishment for some misdeed, to dive to the bottom of the lake. His task was to remove fallen branches and other debris that had collected under the diving board, so that campers could dive safely. In another version of the story, Jacques voluntarily took on the job. The truth, however, may lie in between. The initial dive may have been a punishment, later ones done voluntarily, as Jacques discovered the thrill of being underwater.

Despite Jacques's enthusiasm for activities in the water, it was hard work diving in the muddy water without goggles and without any kind of breathing apparatus. Jacques soon learned to gulp in as much air as his lungs would hold, descend quickly to the bottom to work, and return frequently to the surface to refill his lungs. Already, though, Jacques Cousteau was beginning to think of ways to stay underwater longer. In one adventure story that he had read, the hero escaped from his enemies by hiding on the bottom of a river and breathing through a hollow reed. Adapting this idea, Jacques pushed a length of rubber garden hose through a block of cork so that one end of the hose would float above water. He then descended to the bottom of the lake with the other end of the hose in his mouth. He quickly discovered that he could not suck air through the hose, so just as quickly, he returned to the surface.

Back in New York City, Jacques bubbled over with ideas. Some of them turned into elaborate projects. At the age of 11, he borrowed the blueprints for a 200-ton floating crane and built a 4-foot working model of it. Proud of his son, Daniel Cousteau showed the model to a knowledgeable friend, who believed that an improvement Jacques had added was good enough to be patented. Later, engineers added Jacques's changes to the design of the crane.

In 1922, Higgins and the Cousteaus returned to France, where Jacques continued to devise projects for himself. At age 13, he built a 3-foot-long, battery-operated automobile. That same year, after a family trip to Mexico, Jacques wrote, illustrated, typeset, and bound a book entitled *An Adventure in Mexico*.

Also at 13, he used his allowance to buy one of the first home-movie cameras sold in France, a Pathé. The first thing Jacques did with the Pathé was take it apart and put it back together again. It was an exercise that he would do over and over again. The internal workings of the camera were almost as interesting to him as what he could do with it.

Jacques shot his first home movie at a cousin's wedding. Not long after that, he used his movie camera to record his parents walking up the gangplank of Higgins's yacht, Daniel with a self-conscious smile on his face and Elizabeth clutching her hat on her head. There is even a shot of Higgins, sporting a small pointed beard, standing on the deck with a group of friends.

This woodcut from the 1500s shows a simple underwater breathing apparatus, like the one used in the adventure story Jacques read as a boy.

Filmmaking quickly became Jacques's passion. He loved movies, not only French ones, but also the American comedies of Charlie Chaplin and Buster Keaton. For his own films, he specialized in melodrama, always casting himself as the heartless villain. His father's car, a convertible, was a favorite prop. One of his productions shows the villain—a shifty-eyed Jacques wearing a fake mustache—driving off in the convertible, a young woman at his side. Quickly, the hero gives chase. When the villain stops the car to kiss the heroine, the hero catches up with them. Dragging Jacques from behind the wheel, the hero leaves him on the street and drives off with the woman.

Jacques never minded suffering for the sake of his art. Another Cousteau melodrama shows the heroine of the film rejecting Jacques's advances by pushing him, fully clothed, into the harbor.

Jacques called his amateur film production company Société Zix, and he gave himself credit as producer, director, and chief cameraman of the films. He could not wait to be grown-up and make his own way in the world—much like his admired older brother, who had been allowed to quit school at 16 and go into business.

While Jacques was a model of industriousness with his filmmaking, his enthusiasm did not carry over to formal education. In school, his fellow students viewed him as lazy and a show-off. At one point, Jacques's parents took the Pathé away from him because of his poor grades.

Before Jacques won back the camera, he got into even bigger trouble: He had systematically broken 17 windows in the stairwell of his school. According to one version of the incident, this was the result of a scientific experiment. Jacques was trying to prove that the more forcefully a stone was thrown against glass, the smaller the hole it would make. Another version is that Jacques was merely trying to create the effect seen in American cowboy movies when gunmen shot round holes in saloon windows. Years later, Cousteau commented on his problems at school by claiming to be a "misfit."

Misfit or not, his parents lost patience and sent him off to a very strict boarding school in the Alsace region of France. There he would have to shape up—or else.

A
NAVY
MAN

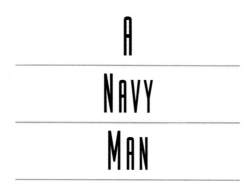

The discipline and challenges provided by the Alsatian boarding school proved to be just what Jacques Cousteau needed. Immediately, there was a radical change in his attitude. There were no more pranks, no more experiments, no more fooling around. His schoolwork came first. Jacques often studied late into the night, taking a book and a flashlight under the covers with him. By the time he graduated in 1929, at age 19, he was a model student.

What would he do next? Three possible careers appealed to him. He could imagine becoming a radiologist. He would relish being a film director, or he could become a naval officer and fulfill his longtime ambition to see the world.

16

In the end, the lure of traveling around the world by ship—and being paid to do it—won out. In 1930, Jacques Cousteau entered the French Naval Academy at Brest, in Brittany, on the western coast of France. A few years later, Cousteau graduated second in his class and entered the French Navy.

In 1932 and 1933, Cousteau and his classmates circumnavigated the globe in the training ship *Jeanne d'Arc.* The dedicated filmmaker took along his Pathé to capture highlights of the voyage. In the Persian Gulf, he recorded the sultan of Oman's visit to the ship. At Angkor Wat, in Cambodia, Cousteau filmed graceful dancers. In Japan, he captured on film the delicate motions of geishas. In the South Seas, the young naval officer watched with wonder from the *Jeanne d'Arc* as pearl divers, clad only in loincloths and cumbersome goggles, dived for oysters.

Across the Pacific, on the West Coast of the United States, Cousteau toured Hollywood. There he met the popular movie actress Claudette Colbert. He also had himself filmed with actor Douglas Fairbanks and his wife, actress Mary Pickford.

After the training voyage, in 1933, Cousteau graduated from the naval academy and was commissioned as a second lieutenant in the French Navy. He was made a gunnery officer and was assigned to a ship berthed in the port of Shanghai, on the mainland China coast. From there, he and his shipmates took part in a mapmaking survey along the Indochina coast. One noon at Port Dayot, Cousteau and others watched as a local fisherman plunged into the water without goggles or diving gear. Shortly, the fisherman surfaced with a wiggling fish in each hand. To the amazed French Navy men Cousteau explained, with a twinkle in his eye, that at that time of day, it was easy to take the fish, because they were napping.

When his tour of duty in the Far East ended, Cousteau received permission to travel back to France on his own. He booked a ticket on the Trans-Siberian Express and made the long train ride through the Soviet Union, with a side trip by car to the Hindu Kush Mountains in Afghanistan. As always, the devoted filmmaker captured the highlights with his camera. The Soviet Union, however, then ruled by Joseph Stalin, was a tightly controlled society, and foreigners were not allowed to take pictures. At the end of the journey, Soviet government officials seized and destroyed most of Cousteau's film.

New Challenges

Back in France, Cousteau embarked on a new adventure: No longer content to see the world from the deck of a ship, he wanted to see it from the air. He enrolled in a naval aviation school at Hourtin, on France's Atlantic coast. The town was only 20 minutes by air from Cousteau's birthplace. While his fellow aviation students spent their spare time having fun, Cousteau enjoyed experimenting with a variety of mechanical devices—and, of course, making films. During training flights, he took his camera with him and shot footage of mock battles between the fighter planes.

Cousteau was due to earn his pilot's license early in 1936. Just a few weeks before his graduation, he was invited to a friend's wedding, to be held in the Vosges Mountains, in northeastern France. Borrowing his father's sports car for the drive to the mountains, Cousteau set off on his lighthearted excursion, completely unaware that he was headed for near-tragedy.

As he drove into the Vosges, night began to fall. Fog reduced the visibility, and Cousteau struggled to maneuver the car around hairpin turns in the winding mountain road. Suddenly, the headlights failed. Cousteau slammed his foot on the brake, but it was too late. The convertible careened off the side of the road and rolled over several times. Then all was still.

For hours, Jacques Cousteau lay unconscious in the woods. No one had seen the accident, and no one came to help. Eventually, at about 2:00 in the morning, he regained consciousness. He had been thrown from the convertible, and his head had been jammed into the ground from the force of the impact. He was bleeding profusely. Twelve of his bones were broken.

In agony, Cousteau managed to crawl to the road; but still no one came. Somehow, he got himself onto his back and looked up at the stars. Fully expecting to die on that mountain road, he thought about how lucky he had been to have seen so many things in his life. But he was not quite ready to give up.

After resting, he convinced himself to continue down the road. Every movement was torture. Finally, he came to a road sign: The nearest village was 4 miles away. Despair overcame him. Then he heard a dog bark. Dragging himself toward the sound, he spied the vague outlines of a small cottage. After hearing Cousteau's cries for help, the residents fetched a doctor.

Later, in the hospital, Cousteau learned the extent of his injuries. Several of his ribs had been crushed, his lungs had been punctured, and his left arm had been broken in five

Toulon, where Cousteau was sent to recover from his injuries, had a harbor that was important to the French Navy. Here battleships are seen in Toulon prior to the start of World War II.

places. Pieces of bone stuck out through the skin, and his right arm was paralyzed.

For several days, he drifted in and out of consciousness. During one of his conscious periods, the doctor told Cousteau that his right arm was infected and would have to be amputated. Cousteau refused. The infection cleared up, but the paralysis remained. Cousteau would not give up. After eight months of whirlpool baths and painful physical therapy, he was able to move one finger on his right hand. Several months after that, he had all five fingers working.

In the meantime, he had been released from the hospital. For his recuperation period, the French Navy ordered him to Toulon, on the Mediterranean Sea. Because of his injuries, Cousteau could not take the pilot's exam that he had been

preparing for. His career as a pilot for the French Navy was over before it could start. Ironically, though, the car accident may have actually saved Jacques Cousteau's life. Almost every other cadet in his flying class died in World War II, which would begin three years later.

Early Dives

Toulon is one of the most sheltered and beautiful harbors on the Mediterranean Sea. Tall hills surround the harbor, and picturesque homes perch on the hillsides. In 1936, when Cousteau reported for duty there, 60 French warships lay at anchor but there was little thought of war. Cousteau was

DIVING DANGERS

Humans who want to dive deep and stay underwater for long periods of time face some very real physical challenges. For one thing, the deeper a diver goes, the greater the pressure on the human body. At 33 feet below the surface of the water, the pressure is twice as great as at the surface; at 66 feet, it is three times as great; and so on. Fortunately, even under great pressure, the human body cannot be compressed—except for the hollow parts. This is why it is important for divers to keep the pressure in the lungs and other air spaces in the body equal to the surrounding water pressure. Otherwise, the diver suffers from a condition known as barotrauma, or squeeze.

The pressure on the body underwater brings about chemical changes in the blood. The air that we breathe on land is made of different chemicals. Four-fifths of it is nitrogen. A diver 33 feet below breathes twice as much air as at the surface to maintain the same pressure in the lungs as in the surrounding sea. Twice as much air means twice as much nitrogen.

Because nitrogen is a heavy inert (chemically inactive) gas, it does not leave the body along with the other gases—mainly carbon dioxide—that a diver breathes out. Instead, it dissolves in the blood and tissues, from which the lungs remove it, and, then, it is breathed out. This is not a problem as long as a diver's body remains under pressure. When the diver starts to ascend to the surface and the pressure decreases, however, the nitrogen forms tiny bubbles in the blood.

assigned to artillery, ammunitions, and gunnery equipment. His most important job, however, was to work on healing his shattered arms.

Soon after his arrival in Toulon, Cousteau met fellow navy officer Philippe Tailliez. Tailliez encouraged him to swim every day to strengthen his arms. When they were off duty,

As the diver rises, the bubbles expand. They start to block off capillaries, then veins, then arteries. In its mildest form, this condition, called decompression sickness, causes extreme pain in the joints. In its most severe form, it can actually kill a diver. Because a diver may bend his or her body into a contorted position to try to relieve the pain in the joints, decompression sickness is also called the bends.

Decompression sickness is not a threat of dives that are very short in duration. But even a diver who has stayed down for a long time can easily avoid decompression sickness by coming up slowly, stopping one or more times to allow the body to rid itself of excess nitrogen through breathing. As a last resort, a diver who has surfaced too quickly can be put in a recompression chamber, which takes the diver's body to the pressure that it was underwater and then slowly reduces the pressure at the proper rate.

Charts called decompression tables tell divers how long they can stay at various depths without absorbing too much nitrogen. The tables also tell how slowly divers should come up in order to avoid decompression sickness.

Nitrogen is responsible for another danger to divers: Those people who dive to extreme depths may experience hallucinations and loss of reasoning, often called "rapture of the deep." Many feel an exaggerated sense of well-being and power. While in this state, a diver may do things that endanger his or her life. This condition is known as nitrogen narcosis. It can be avoided by not going down too deep or by breathing a mixture of gases that includes helium in place of nitrogen.

the two could usually be found in the clear, blue waters of the Mediterranean.

Prolonged swimming in salt water introduced Cousteau to two frustrating facts about human eyes and water: Salt water stings the eyes, and when opened underwater, the naked human eye is almost blind. For centuries, those who made a living by diving—pearl divers, coral divers, sponge divers—had used various forms of underwater goggles to increase their efficiency.

One day, Tailliez presented Cousteau with a pair of goggles made by the Fernez company, only recently available for sale in France. The result was startling. Opening his eyes underwater, Cousteau saw a whole new world—rocks covered with forests of algae, and strange fish swimming all around him. When he stood up in the shallow water to take in air, he could look toward shore and see the life he knew so well—a trolley car, people, electric-light poles. The next moment, he was submerged again in a marvelous world unknown to those who had never penetrated its boundaries.

Cousteau reveled in the beauty of the underwater vistas newly available to him through the Fernez goggles. He also found a new world on the land. One weekend during his period of recuperation, Cousteau visited his parents in Paris. While there, he was invited to a party. One of the other guests was a slim, 17-year-old student named Simone Melchior. Cousteau, now 26, was immediately attracted to her. He had, of course, brought his camera to the party. With it, he captured Simone sitting among a group of friends and shyly announcing her name to the cameraman.

Simone Melchoir came from a navy family; her father was a retired admiral. When the attraction between Cousteau and their daughter became obvious, the Melchior family decided that Cousteau was a promising suitor. They insisted, however, that Simone finish school before any wedding could take place.

For the next year, whenever Cousteau could get leave from the navy, he traveled to Paris to be with her. His persistence paid off. On July 12, 1937, Jacques-Yves Cousteau and Simone Melchior were married in a formal wedding. The groom wore his navy dress uniform and the bride was beautiful in a full-length white gown. Together, they marched out of the church under the unsheathed swords of Cousteau's navy comrades.

The newlyweds moved into a house in Sanary, a community of officers' quarters near the Toulon naval base. Simone, also a lover of the water, frequently swam with her husband and Philippe Tailliez in their continuing exploration of the Mediterranean's underwater delights.

Cousteau and Tailliez were not the only ones who preferred the sea to land. In the waters around Toulon was a group of men who fished with an odd array of weapons, including spears, spring guns, fencing foils, and bows and arrows. One of the underwater hunters was Frédéric ("Didi") Dumas, a champion spear fisherman. Soon after Cousteau and Tailliez met Dumas, the three embarked on a continuing attempt to make themselves more at home in the water. Their goals were to stay underwater longer, to dive deeper, and to see more. They wanted to be at home in the underwater world—they wanted to be what they referred to as "menfish."

MENFISH

In the late 1930s, as Cousteau and his friends Philippe Tailliez and Frédéric Dumas spent more and more time in the water, they began to experiment with ways of making their hobby more comfortable and more fun. As it turned out, they found ways to make diving more than just a hobby as well.

Diving goggles had opened their eyes to the riches of the sea, but they found that goggles also had drawbacks. One disadvantage was the difficulty of keeping both of the goggle lenses in the same plane, or level. A slight shift in the position of one lens could distort what was being seen.

Another drawback of goggles was the effect of water pressure, which could flatten the lenses against the eyes.

A one-piece glass mask that covered both eyes and nose solved these two problems. The mask allowed both eyes to look through the same plane, and it used the diver's nose to keep the glass from flattening against the eyes. Cousteau and his friends did not invent the one-piece diving mask, but they did show ingenuity in fashioning such masks from old inner tubes. At the same time, in order to keep their faces below the surface of the water for longer periods, they created snorkel-like breathing tubes from garden hoses. Eventually, they added foot flippers to their diving gear, allowing them to swim more easily and freeing their hands for other things, such as underwater filming.

Naturally, Cousteau wanted to capture his new undersea experiences on film. For his first attempt at filming the sea, he made a waterproof casing for his camera. A clothespin served as a lever that could be manipulated to change the focus of the lens. As his first subject, Cousteau chose to film Dumas spearfishing. The primitive underwater camera worked, but the limitations of the device were frustrating— Cousteau had to resurface every 30 seconds to rewind the mechanism.

Cousteau, Tailliez, and Dumas took a scientific approach to diving and experimented on themselves. They wanted to learn all they could about the human body in the underwater environment. Cousteau was especially sensitive to cold water, so they started their research by studying ways to keep warm.

To their surprise, they learned that swimmers who coated themselves with grease were not helping themselves. Grease washes off in the water and leaves a thin layer of oil, which actually causes the swimmer's body to lose some heat. They also learned what not to do after a dive. Wrapping themselves in blankets did not really warm them. Because the body tries to keep its central temperature constant, it lets heat drain off the outer layer first in the water. Covering the body with blankets forces the body to burn up more calories sending heat to the outer layer of skin and away from vital organs. Drinking warm liquids or alcohol also did nothing to heat the surface of the body. What did help, they learned, was to submerge the body in hot water or to stand between two roaring fires on the beach.

While these experiments on different methods of getting warm were helpful, they did not address the real problem of how to stay warm underwater. Cousteau soon took to fashioning diving garments out of rubber, but all his creations had weaknesses. One model could be inflated slightly to allow more insulating air around the skin. This positive feature, however, was offset by the fact that the suit worked at only one depth, and Cousteau had to spend most of his time resisting the forces that tried to pull him up or down in the water. The inflatable suit had another disadvantage: The air inside the suit tended to move to the feet and force Cousteau into a head-down position.

Despite such setbacks, they kept working on diving suits. However, it was not until eight years later that Cousteau and his partners developed a workable solution to the problem of keeping warm in cold water. In 1946, they devised a constant-volume suit. The diver inflated it by breathing out through the nose under the edge of an inner mask. Excess air could be let out through escape valves located at the head, wrists, and ankles. This allowed the diver to remain stable at any depth and in any position.

Jacques Cousteau

Diving suits—like this one worn by people diving for amber—
had been used since the mid-1800s, but they were bulky.
Cousteau set out to revolutionize the diving suit.

Protection from the cold water was important, but the divers' main concern was how to stay underwater longer with complete freedom of movement. They were not at all interested in the awkward diving suits that had been in use since the mid-1800s. Divers using such suits were not only bound to the surface by their air lines, but their sight and their movements were also severely limited by the heavy suits and helmets.

Cousteau, Tailliez, and Dumas wanted to be like the 60-year-old Arab sponge diver whom Cousteau had seen on an island off Tunisia in North Africa, in 1939. Without any breathing apparatus, the diver had descended to a depth of 130 feet and stayed under for an impressive two-and-a-half minutes. (Most breath-holding divers must surface in less than one minute.) Those people who dived for sponges and pearls began training for such feats as young children; Cousteau and his friends were starting their training as adults. Nonetheless, their determination brought victory. Before long, they had accustomed their bodies to diving to 60 feet—the average depth reached by sponge divers—and staying underwater for two minutes.

But for Jacques Cousteau, this was not long enough. In two minutes, Cousteau could catch only brief glimpses of the undersea world that he so longed to know. He wanted to stay longer, and the only way to do that was to use an underwater breathing device. He tried out Yves Le Prieur's compressed-air device, invented in 1926, but found it lacking. The device provided no way of regulating the air flow, so the air was soon used up. To Cousteau, this was not much better than diving without a breathing apparatus. More and more, it seemed to him that he would have to create his own equipment for breathing underwater.

Cousteau's frustration with Le Prieur's compressed-air device led him to experiment with oxygen. Soon he had designed a breathing apparatus that let the diver reuse spent oxygen. The gunsmith on Cousteau's ship constructed the device to Cousteau's specifications. Using a canister of soda lime from a gas mask, a bottle of oxygen, and a length of inner tube from a motorbike, the gunsmith fashioned an artificial lung that could be worn around the waist. When the diver exhaled air containing carbon dioxide, the soda lime repurified carbon dioxide so that it was, once again, breathable oxygen. The oxygen could thus be breathed over and over again, allowing the diver to stay down for long periods of time.

Cousteau had been told that it was safe to breathe oxygen down to a depth of 45 feet. Lower than that, a diver would have an oxygen convulsion and lose consciousness.

For a test run of the oxygen rebreathing device, two sailors from Cousteau's ship rowed him out into the harbor. They watched as he strapped on the artificial lung and dived into the water.

With his legs clamped together and his arms at his side, Cousteau descended with the rippling motions of a fish, and the fish accepted him into their midst. A group of silver and gold giltheads with scarlet gill patches let him swim along with them. But this "fish swimming" was too slow for Cousteau. He could swim faster by kicking his flippered feet, which he now did. Immediately, the fish recognized him as a "foreigner." Cousteau chased one into an underwater cave, and it bristled its dorsal fin and rolled its eyes.

Then Cousteau spotted a large fish motionless about 45 feet down. Here was the test of oxygen's limits. Cousteau headed down. Suddenly, his lips began to tremble. His eyelids blinked uncontrollably. His spine went backward. He realized he was having an oxygen convulsion. In his last few seconds of consciousness, he ripped off the 10-pound weight clamped around his waist, and his unconscious body floated to the surface. The two sailors pulled him out of the water. Eventually, Cousteau regained consciousness, but for weeks afterward, his neck hurt and his muscles ached.

Cousteau was convinced that problems with the design of the rebreathing device had brought on the oxygen convulsion. He spent the winter improving the mechanism. The next summer, he went back to the same spot and, with the new oxygen lung, dived to 45 feet. This time, the convulsion came on so quickly that, afterward, when he had been pulled from the water and revived, Cousteau could not even recall removing his weights. Disgusted, and unwilling to risk his life again, Cousteau gave up on oxygen. Only later did he learn that there was nothing wrong with his design. The experts had been wrong: Oxygen can be deadly at just 33—not 45—feet.

Cousteau's failure to create an underwater breathing apparatus with either compressed air or oxygen did not stop him from diving. In the summer of 1939, off the coast of Tunisia, he was underwater by himself when he noticed a flat, stony floor 30 feet down. Closer inspection revealed that it was a false floor—there were holes in it big enough to swim through. Looking through one of them, Cousteau saw that the "floor" was actually a platform held up by natural pillars. The true sandy ocean bottom lay 3 feet below.

Fueled by curiosity, he decided to swim in through one hole and back out through another about 50 feet away. He knew that he could hold his breath for two minutes, and he estimated that he could swim the distance between the two holes at a leisurely pace in 40 seconds. This would give him time to get down to the depth of the holes, swim through one hole and over to the other one, and get back up to the surface.

At first, everything proceeded as planned. When Cousteau got to the second hole, however, he could not get his shoulders through it. He had 30 seconds left to breathe— not enough time to get back to the first hole. Suddenly, he saw a third hole that he had not noticed before. He pushed his body through the hole, but the stony rim cut him badly.

After he surfaced, Cousteau realized how foolish he had been to attempt the dive without more careful advanced planning. Even more important was the realization that he still wanted a breathing apparatus that would let him avoid such narrow escapes altogether. He thought that he would try working with compressed air again—but his experiments were soon interrupted by world events.

War!

Tension had long been building between Nazi Germany and most of its European neighbors. When Germany invaded Poland in September 1939, England and France immediately declared war on Germany and its ally, Italy. Jacques Cousteau was aboard his ship in the Algerian port of Oran when war broke out. Also in the harbor was a French torpedo boat, which was useless because a heavy steel cable was twisted around its screw propeller.

Learning of the disabled torpedo boat, Cousteau recruited five other divers from his naval ship, the *Dupleix*, to try to free the propeller screw from the cable. For several hours,

Cousteau was stationed aboard the *Dupleix*, a French Navy ship, when World War II broke out.

the six of them dived repeatedly, coming up every two minutes for a lungful of air. Finally, they had cut all the steel cable away from the screw. The divers were so exhausted that they could hardly stand up.

Before this time, Cousteau's dives had always been for fun. Now, though, he understood the difficulty of doing hard work underwater without breathing apparatus. Once again, he renewed his commitment to create an underwater breathing apparatus—not only for enjoyment but also for essential work.

For several months at the beginning of the war, Cousteau was busy with his naval duties. He had been made gunnery officer on the *Dupleix*. In May-June 1940, German forces invaded and occupied the north of France. The defeated French surrendered to Adolf Hitler, leader of Nazi Germany.

For a while, the Germans did not occupy the south of France. In November 1942, however, German forces attacked the naval base at Toulon. French naval officials had been ready for this possibility for two years. Every ship in the Mediterranean fleet had been wired with explosives.

Rather than see their ships fall into the hands of the Germans, the French blew up every single one of their ships. Cousteau and Simone wept by the radio as they listened to Radio Geneva report on the event.

Although they grieved deeply for their country, Jacques and Simone Cousteau had some happy times during the war. Home movies taken at the time show them cheerfully playing games with their two young sons—Jean-Michel, born in March 1938, and Philippe, born in December 1939.

Even after the French fleet was destroyed, the Cousteaus, Frédéric Dumas, and Philippe Tailliez continued their diving experiments in the waters near Toulon. Food was scarce during the war, and many of the dives were given over to spearing fish, the mainstay of their diet. But other dives were purely experimental.

By now, Fernez had come out with a compressed-air underwater breathing device. It consisted of a tube connected to tanks of compressed air and a pump on the surface of the water. Through a mouthpiece, a diver was able to suck in as much compressed air as was needed. The device, however, had certain drawbacks. It wasted half the air, and it limited the diver's movements because he or she was always attached to the surface. Still, Cousteau found it better than anything else he had used.

Then, one day when Cousteau was diving with the Fernez pump, he felt a sudden shock in his lungs. Immediately, he stopped inhaling and held his breath. He tugged on the air tube. It came down without resistance, revealing that it had broken near the surface. If Cousteau had kept breathing, he would have inhaled noncompressed air from the surface, and the force of water pressure would have collapsed his lungs. As it was, he suffered no ill effects from the incident.

When Dumas had a similar accident, however, the divers became convinced that they needed something more reliable than the Fernez pump.

While they experimented with various ideas for underwater breathing devices, Cousteau, Dumas, and Tailliez remained interested in underwater photography. During the war, they made their first film, *Sixty Feet Down* (also known as *Through 18 Meters of Water*).

The film was made without breathing apparatus or modern photographic equipment. They didn't have lights or a waterproof camera. In fact, film for movie cameras was so scarce that Cousteau bought several rolls of film for stills, and he and Simone spliced the rolls together, working under the darkness of blankets at night to avoid exposing the film to any light. Shooting was limited to two-minute segments because both the cameraman (Cousteau) and his subject (Dumas) had to hold their breath underwater. Working in this way, they were able to create an 18-minute film that captures the drama of Dumas spearing a grouper in an underwater tunnel.

Cousteau and his friends carried out their filming and their diving experiments under the watchful eye of German and Italian patrols in the Mediterranean. Fortunately, the enemy soldiers thought that these divers, with their homemade diving and underwater photography equipment, were harmless oddballs. The divers did their best to reinforce this impression.

In reality, however, Cousteau was far from being harmless to the enemy. In fact, he worked with the French resistance movement, which was determined to rid France of its German and Italian occupiers. Spending so much time in and near the water, Cousteau was able to provide the resistance with detailed notes on the movements of German and Italian ships in the area.

Some of his spying put him in great danger. One night, he went ashore at Sète, an enemy-occupied spot on the French coast. Posing as an Italian naval officer, Cousteau obtained entrance to Italian naval headquarters. There he spent four hours taking photographs of the enemy code book with a miniature camera. The Allies (Great Britain, the United States, and the Free French forces) used the information that Cousteau gathered to decode the Italian naval signals before the Allied invasion of North Africa. For his efforts, after the war, Cousteau received the Légion d'Honneur (Legion of Honor)—France's highest military and civilian honor.

THE AQUALUNG

Everything that Cousteau wanted to do—explore the ocean freely, help his country win the war, make underwater films—could be done more easily with a self-contained underwater breathing apparatus that did not bind a diver to the surface. Others had experimented with the idea, and Cousteau had tried out many of their experiments. The most successful had been Le Prieur's compressed-air apparatus. It required the diver to control the flow of air with a hand-held valve, however, and it used up air too quickly. Cousteau wanted his hands free, and he wanted to use compressed air as efficiently as possible.

The solution seemed to be an automatic regulator that would feed compressed air to a diver without the diver having to think about it. Airplane pilots flying at high altitudes already had a similar device in their oxygen masks that responded to their needs for oxygen on demand. Now that Cousteau knew exactly what he wanted, he realized that he needed the help of an expert to design it. Who could help him?

Jacques Cousteau had heard of an engineer named Émile Gagnan who specialized in handling gases under pressure. Gagnan worked in Paris for an international firm called Air Liquide. By chance, Cousteau's father-in-law, retired admiral Melchior, was one of the directors of Air Liquide. Melchior convinced his fellow directors that it would be worthwhile to let Gagnan work on his son-in-law's project. In December 1942, Cousteau and his wife, Simone, traveled to Nazi-occupied Paris to meet with Gagnan. (Their children were with Cousteau's mother in Megeve, near the Italian-Swiss border.)

Cousteau outlined his requirements for an underwater breathing apparatus to Gagnan. The engineer showed Cousteau a small plastic device that he had designed. Gasoline was so scarce in wartime France that engineers had been working on all kinds of projects to find alternative sources of fuel. In Gagnan's solution, cooking gas was carried in a tank on top of the car, and a valve regulated the flow of gas to the engine. Gagnan's creative mind was able to see the connection between the automatic regulator that he had designed and what Cousteau was looking for.

For a few weeks, Cousteau and Gagnan worked together in the Air Liquide laboratories. Their goal was to produce a regulating valve that would automatically supply a diver with air at the right pressure for the diver's depth. The device had to be sensitive enough to respond to human breath, so that when a diver inhaled, the regulator would release just the right amount of air from the tank; and when the diver exhaled, the regulator would close off the air tank and let the exhaled air escape into the water.

By January 1943, Gagnan and Cousteau thought they had what they needed. The rig consisted of a mouthpiece connected to two hoses. The hoses wound around to the back of the body, where they connected to the regulator, which in turn was connected to tanks of compressed air. The regulator had a wet chamber and a dry chamber, with a diaphragm, or flexible wall, between the two. The hose that delivered air to the diver was connected to the dry chamber. When the diver inhaled, the air pressure in the dry chamber decreased, and the diaphragm was sucked in. This caused two levers to open and send air from the tank into the dry chamber, restoring the diaphragm to its former position and stopping the air supply. Now the pressure in the dry chamber was the same as the pressure in the surrounding sea and in the diver's lungs, and the air could be breathed safely by the diver. The diver exhaled through the same mouthpiece. The stale air passed out of the other hose and into the sea through a one-way valve.

Cousteau and Gagnan now tested their device in the Marne River outside Paris. Cousteau, clad only in a bathing suit and his diving gear, entered the icy waters and disappeared. For a while, bubbles reached the surface. The device was working. Then the bubbles stopped. Gagnan began to worry, but Cousteau finally surfaced. He was not happy at all. When he had been swimming horizontally, the lung worked fine. But when he stood up underwater, air rushed out of the exhaust valve and was wasted; and when he was head-down in the water, he could not breathe. What was the use of a lung that would not let you go up and down in the water?

Soon Cousteau and Gagnan realized the cause of the problem: they had placed the exhaust valve in the mouthpiece, which made it 10 inches higher than the regulator. Underwater, 10 inches made a big difference in the water pressure. When Cousteau was standing underwater, the stale air leaving the exhaust valve was at a lower pressure than the air being taken in, so too much air was rushing into the dry chamber and flowing out of the exhaust. When he was upside down, the exhaust valve was 10 inches lower in the water and under greater pressure than the intake, so it was hard for Cousteau to expel stale air and take in fresh air.

Elated, the partners returned to the lab. With a few simple adjustments, they had the exhaust and intake valves close together. It was time for another tryout. This time they went to an indoor water tank in Paris. Cousteau dove in and immediately began doing underwater acrobatics. The lung worked perfectly in any position. With their invention, Jacques Cousteau and Émile Gagnan had freed humans to swim with the fishes. Cousteau returned to the south of France while Gagnan put the finishing touches on their new invention, which they called the aqualung.

The Real Test

In June 1943, Gagnan shipped a finished aqualung to Cousteau in Toulon. The Cousteaus, Tailliez, and Dumas unwrapped the package with all the excitement of children on Christmas morning. Immediately, they rushed to a quiet spot on the beach.

Cousteau donned his face mask, flippers, and the aqualung. Dumas stayed on the beach so that he would be

PIONEERS IN UNDERWATER BREATHING

In order for humans to stay alive underwater, they, of course, must find a way to breathe. One way is to fill one's lungs before descending and then slowly exhale underwater. People in warm seas have been doing this for thousands of years. The ancient Greek philosopher Aristotle wrote so accurately about fish that some scholars believe that he was a diver. Early European explorers of the Caribbean reported that the Lucayans—inhabitants of the Bahamas—fished underwater with spears and dived for pearls. But free diving has definite limits. Even the most experienced divers can go no deeper than 100 feet and are limited to two minutes underwater.

Looking for ways to stay underwater longer, divers began to experiment with breathing air through pipes or tubes that connected them to the surface. The brilliant Italian artist and inventor Leonardo da Vinci (1452–1519) designed a leather diving helmet with windows. A long tube connected the helmet to the surface. In the early 1700s, several English inventors developed diving suits and helmets of wood and leather. In 1715, John Lethbridge constructed a diving suit that he called a "divine engine." It was a 6-foot-long, watertight wooden case with two holes for the diver's arms and a glass porthole at one end for the diver to look through. With the diver inside, the box was lowered into the water by ropes. Air was pumped down to the diver through a tube. Lethbridge claimed to have gone down to 60 feet and to have stayed for half an hour in the device.

The first practical diving suit and helmet were designed in 1819 by Augustus Siebe, a German inventor living in England. This suit had weighted shoes to let the diver stand upright. But, the suit had a major drawback—the jacket was open at the bottom and depended on the air pressure inside the suit to keep out the water. If the diver fell, the air would rush out and be replaced with water and the diver could drown. Eighteen years later, Siebe improved his original design by making a closed suit that no water could penetrate. His basic design is still used today.

Diving suits were extremely useful for divers working underwater for long periods of time, but they restricted divers' movements because they could not venture farther than the tubes would allow.

As far back as 1825, scientists began to look for ways that divers could carry their air supply with them. The first useful system was built in 1865 by two Frenchmen, Benoit Rouquayrol and Auguste Denayrouze. The system required divers to wear a metal cylinder of air on their back but allowed them to go down to 165 feet. Because scientists had not yet devised a way of compressing air sufficiently, though, the tanks had to be very large, or the dives had to be too brief.

By 1926, compressed air was available, and Frenchman Yves Le Prieur used it in the underwater breathing system that he devised. In his system, a diver regulated the flow of air by a hand-held valve, and much of the air rushed out, wasted, when the diver exhaled. Le Prieur was on the right track, but something more was needed. The person, or persons, who could invent an efficient automatic regulator for a self-contained underwater breathing apparatus—SCUBA—would be the hero of divers everywhere.

These diving suits from the 1870s were quite awkward to use.

warm and rested if anything went wrong and he needed to go to Cousteau's aid. Simone put on a face mask and snorkel. She would watch her husband from the surface and signal Dumas if anything was amiss.

When all were in place, Cousteau plunged into the sea. With a kick and a glide, a kick and a glide, he reached a depth of 30 feet. The aqualung functioned perfectly, feeding him air compressed to exactly the right pressure for each new depth he reached. Convinced that he need not worry about his equipment, Cousteau began to play. He performed loops, somersaults, and barrel rolls; upside down, he balanced on one finger.

Fifteen minutes went by. Cousteau had enough air for an hour and would stay under as long as he could stand the cold. Tunnels that before he had only been able to glimpse now beckoned. He glided down one and found himself in a cave with a low ceiling. Trying to avoid scraping his air tanks on the roof of the cave, Cousteau turned over onto his back. To his surprise, he beheld dozens of lobsters clinging to the ceiling of the cave, waving their antennae. Cousteau harvested several loads of lobster and delivered them to Simone, waiting on the surface. This was a treasure indeed for those reduced to the dull and sparse diet of wartime rations.

Scooping two lobsters from the roof of the cave, Cousteau rose toward the surface. Simone swam down to meet him and took the lobsters. While her husband dove for more, Simone deposited the lobsters on a rock occupied by a lone fisherman. With a smile, she asked the astonished fisherman to watch the lobsters for her. Then she returned to meet Cousteau coming up with the next load. When several more lobsters had been harvested in the same manner, Simone retrieved the lot from the rock and presented the bewildered fisherman with one of the prizes.

That night, the diving friends feasted on lobster and rejoiced in their newfound undersea freedom. They had achieved their goal—they were truly menfish.

During the rest of the summer of 1943, Cousteau, Dumas, and Tailliez made 500 separate dives with the aqualung. By autumn, they had been down to 130 feet, and they wanted to go deeper. In October, the divers decided that Dumas would be the one to go for the record. The group prepared a guide rope, knotted at regular intervals. This rope would help Dumas get down and back and would measure how far he had gone.

On the appointed day, Cousteau jumped into the water first and went down 100 feet to wait for his friend. Dumas plunged. As he later reported, at some point below 100 feet, he began to feel "drunk and carefree." He was also sleepy, but was unable to sleep because of the dizziness. He continued to descend. At last, reaching for one of the knots, he tied his belt to it. This would mark his lowest depth. Then he slowly began the ascent.

At a certain depth, the sensation of drunkenness disappeared. It was replaced by a feeling of depression, as Dumas became convinced that he had gone only slightly below 100 feet. The rope, however, told the true story. Dumas had been 210 feet below the surface! The record depth had affected his ability to think clearly.

Cousteau, Dumas, and Tailliez quickly termed the feeling of intense well-being that Dumas had experienced "rapture of the deep." Later, when Cousteau experienced it for himself, he both loved it and feared it. It was a feeling of great happiness, but under its spell, a diver felt invulnerable and was capable of such madness as tearing out the mouthpiece of the aqualung and offering it to a passing fish.

Later, the French divers learned that U.S. Navy scientists had studied rapture of the deep a few years earlier, but because of the war, reports of their research had not reached occupied France. The navy scientists called it nitrogen narcosis, because it happened when the excess of nitrogen in the blood affected the nervous system. Unlike the bends, which also results from excess nitrogen in the blood, the sensations related to nitrogen narcosis are pleasant, and its effects disappear as soon as the diver returns to shallower water. It is dangerous, however, because it interferes with clear thinking.

As 1943 came to an end and 1944 began, Cousteau, Dumas, and Tailliez continued their underwater adventures. Their newest enthusiasm was exploring sunken ships. Soon they were embarked on another filming project. With the approval of the German occupiers and their Italian allies, they made *Wrecks*, the first underwater film done with the help of the aqualung.

Jacques Cousteau was doing what he had dreamed of for years—he was a manfish. Not only that, he was a filmmaking manfish. World War II still raged in his homeland but soon would come to an end. Jacques Cousteau would then be able to pursue his lifelong dreams with a more single-minded devotion.

UNDERWATER
EXPLORATION

On June 6, 1944—D Day—British, U.S., and other Allied forces landed on the beaches of Normandy in northern France. Within two and a half months, they had liberated Paris from the German occupation army. Like all other French servicemen, Cousteau and Tailliez were called back to duty now that occupation was over. They gladly returned to Toulon to help the French Navy rebuild its fleet. With them they took Dumas, the aqualung, and their enthusiasm for underwater exploration.

At the Toulon shipyard, it took a while for returning officers to get things organized. In the meantime, the three divers took over an abandoned German bomb shelter and hung up a sign: Undersea Research Group. Without official approval, they began to ask sailors returning to duty if they wanted to join. Some said yes.

When the war in Europe ended in May 1945, the navy assigned Cousteau to a dull desk job in Marseilles. Frustrated, Cousteau went to see an admiral and told him about the Undersea Research Group. The admiral was a bit surprised that this unofficial group was operating as part of the French Navy, but after listening to Cousteau talk, he thought that the group might be able to do some useful work. The Undersea Research Group thus became an official branch of the French Navy. Tailliez, who held a higher military rank than Cousteau, was put in charge.

Not long afterward, Cousteau showed some admirals the film *Wrecks*. Impressed with the divers' work, the admirals decided that the Undersea Research Group should focus on minesweeping—removing unexploded mines that the Germans and Italians had laid in the Mediterranean Sea during the war. They were also assigned to retrieve cargo from the French ships that had been sunk during the war. In addition, the admirals agreed that undersea research might be a useful occupation for the group.

The group was given a ship and the job of clearing the Sète harbor of mines. To speed up the job, Cousteau designed an underwater sled on which a diver could be towed. With the sled, a diver could travel three times farther on a tank of air than without a sled. Within five weeks, the group had cleared the harbor; it would have taken helmeted divers several months to do the same job.

Although the Undersea Research Group took much of his attention, Cousteau found time to be with his family. Shortly after the war ended, he built mini-aqualungs for his two sons and gave them their first diving lesson. Their responses, perhaps, were not exactly what Cousteau had in mind, but it did show that the boys were just as enthusiastic about the ocean as their father was. Instead of paying attention to his serious instruction, Jean-Michel and Philippe immediately pushed their faces underwater and began to exclaim about the wonders they could see for the first time. Of course, as soon as the boys opened their mouths to talk, their mouthpieces fell out and they took in a fair amount of salt water. This introduction to the aqualung did not dampen their spirits, however. The two were soon diving like experts and catching octopuses and other sea creatures with their bare hands. A favorite photograph of Jacques Cousteau's taken at the time shows all four Cousteaus standing in the Mediterranean and holding hands.

The family would not always be this close. As the boys grew older, Jacques and Simone Cousteau were away from home for longer periods so that Cousteau could pursue his dreams of worldwide underwater adventures. Jean-Michel and Philippe were sent to boarding school. The boys spent holidays and vacations with their parents, if Jacques and Simone were anywhere near France. If not, Jean-Michel and Philippe would stay with their grandparents. Later, Cousteau would say that he wished he had spent more time with his sons when they were growing up.

PUSHING THE LIMITS

Throughout the late 1940s, the Undersea Research Group continued its minesweeping duties. Whenever possible, however, Cousteau directed the Undersea Research Group toward underwater experiments. Some of the experiments were downright dangerous, as the group pushed the limits of the field.

Perhaps because of their involvement in minesweeping, the divers were particularly fascinated with the effects of underwater explosions. Dumas once hurled a grenade into the water to see how many dead fish would float to the surface and how many would sink. When the grenade did not explode right away, he went to investigate. The grenade exploded right under him, sending shock waves through his body. Miraculously, Dumas was unhurt. When Cousteau checked the tables on underwater explosions, he discovered that an explosion of the magnitude that Dumas had experienced could have killed a diver wearing a helmet and suit. The divers concluded that perhaps an unsuited diver could resist shock better than a suited diver. But a hypothesis was not good enough; they wanted firm answers. Filled with curiosity, and at the same time recognizing the folly of their actions, the divers performed several experiments to test the hypothesis. They found out how close a diver could be to an explosion without suffering permanent damage.

They also kept pushing themselves deeper into the sea. In 1947, Cousteau set a world's record for free diving when he went down to 300 feet. On this dive, he experienced nitrogen narcosis for the first time. When he started his ascent, he noticed that the effects stopped at 260 feet. Through this and other experiments, the divers were rapidly compiling information that would be useful to all future divers.

They also studied the effects of increased pressure on the human body. They knew that at 33 feet below, the body experienced twice as much pressure as at the surface and that the pressure kept increasing as they descended. They were surprised to discover that as the diver went deeper, the pressure changes became easier on the body, so that between 33 and 66 feet, the diver experienced only half as much change as occurred between zero and 33 feet.

Most important, the divers devised tables that showed how often and how long a diver should stop on the way up from a deep dive to avoid the bends. This depended on the length of the dive and on how many other dives the individual had made that day.

One day in the fall of 1947, tragedy struck. Maurice Fargues, a naval officer who had joined the Undersea Research Group after the war ended, descended to a depth of 390 feet. It was well below the boundary where nitrogen narcosis was known to set in. Cousteau had taken safety precautions: Fargues was to tug on a line connected to the boat at regular intervals. Suddenly, however, the signals stopped. The safety man immediately jumped into the water. He found Fargues at 150 feet, his mouthpiece resting on his chest. Rapture of the deep had robbed him of his life.

Fargues's untimely death temporarily discouraged the divers from further depth experiments. It also made Cousteau think about other ways of exploring the ocean's depths, such as by using underwater vehicles. In 1948, he and the Undersea Research Group had a chance to work with one of these vehicles. Called a bathyscaphe, it was the brainchild of a Swiss professor, August Piccard, who hoped to descend to 13,000 feet—five times deeper than anyone had ever dived, and 25 times deeper than submarines normally cruised.

The Undersea Research Group was part of the team that launched the bathyscaphe. On November 26, 1948, the bathyscaphe made a test run lasting 16 minutes. Piccard and

Cousteau eventually built a much safer shark cage than the one he had made in 1948. Here, his cage design is shown in a 1992 television episode of *Odyssey*.

one other person were aboard. All went well, though it took a total of seven hours to launch and retrieve the vessel. Later, the bathyscaphe made a deeper test dive without anyone aboard. The vehicle reached 4,600 feet, but it was severely damaged by mild ocean swells when it surfaced.

Although Cousteau was disappointed that he had not been chosen to descend in the bathyscaphe, the project was good for the Undersea Research Group. It marked the group's first opportunity to work in the Atlantic Ocean. For the occasion, Cousteau built an antishark cage to protect the divers. It was one of his few failures as an inventor. When the cage was hoisted off the deck of the ship, swung out over the side, and then lowered into the ocean, the three occupants—Cousteau, Tailliez, and Dumas—were tossed from side to side and floor to ceiling. Their heads and feet banged painfully on the iron bars. Still, they survived the descent.

While they were submerged, they observed a 6-foot barracuda swim past them. To their chagrin, they noticed that the barracuda could have easily swum right through the iron bars—and so probably could a shark! Not surprisingly, this particular antishark cage was never used again.

Cousteau was steadily gaining recognition as a pioneer underwater filmmaker. Right after the war, he had entered his first film, *Sixty Feet Down*, in the new Cannes Film Festival. Critics and audiences praised it, and Cousteau sold the film to a distributor. Like his film *Wrecks*, which had so impressed the navy admirals, *Sixty Feet Down* was in black and white.

In 1948, Cousteau started experimenting with underwater filming in color. Earlier, he and his divers had learned that colors were not always what they seemed underwater. Once Dumas had killed an 80-pound fish with a dagger. He and Cousteau were startled to see green blood run out of the fish. Convinced that they had discovered a rare phenomenon, they began to haul the fish to the surface. At 55 feet, the flowing blood turned brown. At 20 feet, it was pink, and at the surface it became bright red. The phenomenon, it turned out, was not in the blood; rather, the underwater environment distorts one's perception of color.

To learn more about underwater color, Cousteau took a scientific approach. He and the other divers spent months photographing color charts underwater at various depths. Once they knew how various depths affected one's concept of different colors, they worked on developing artificial lighting techniques that would correct for color distortions. Cousteau's first color filming was lighted by incandescent light, powered through a cable from the surface. To free himself from reliance on the cable, Cousteau next tried a magnesium flare. When this proved dangerous to handle, he developed lighting fed by portable silver and zinc batteries.

Another problem with underwater filming was keeping the camera light enough to be maneuvered easily underwater. Since humans were able to adjust to the greater pressure under the water by breathing compressed air from an aqualung, Cousteau reasoned that feeding compressed air to the camera would make it adjust in weight to the water pressure at different depths. Keeping the camera under the same pressure as the surrounding water made it almost weightless and easier to handle. Thus, he attached a miniature aqualung to a camera. Before descending, the diver opened a valve that automatically adjusted the intake of air into the camera's waterproof case.

In 1950, the Undersea Research Group moved into a new building in the Toulon shipyard. It was a state-of-the art diving center, complete with compression chambers, a machine shop, photo lab, containers for captured marine animals, a conference center, and a diving well that could duplicate the kind of pressure found 800 feet underwater.

Cousteau, however, was not content. He wanted to be captain of his own research ship, separate from the navy's chain of command. But how could a navy officer afford to buy a ship?

CALYPSO

A twist of fate provided the answer to Cousteau's dilemma. During the war, Jacques and Simone Cousteau had met a wealthy British couple. The two men had talked all night about the requirements for the ideal oceanic research vessel.

They agreed to keep in touch after the war. In 1950, his wartime acquaintance offered Cousteau the money to buy a surplus minesweeper and to refit it as an oceanographic research vessel.

Cousteau found his dream ship on the island of Malta, south of Sicily. Built in Seattle, Washington, during World War II, the sturdy minesweeper had been turned into a car and passenger ferry after the war. The new owners had renamed it *Calypso,* for the beautiful sea nymph whose charms kept the legendary Greek warrior Odysseus on her island for seven years.

Cousteau took possession of *Calypso* on July 19, 1950. The ship was owned by Cousteau's newly formed nonprofit organization, Campagnes Océanographiques Françaises (French Oceanographic Expeditions).

Cousteau's first job was to remake *Calypso* into a modern research ship. Workers stripped the ship to its bare bones, enlarged the crew quarters, installed a crane on the deck for raising and lowering things into the sea, and installed the most up-to-date navigational aids. Cousteau, Tailliez, and Dumas had been thinking for a long time about what their ideal research vessel would contain. Now they saw some of their dreams come true. Workers built an observation room at the front of the ship, below the waterline. Five portholes allowed for close observation and filming of the undersea environment. Next, the workers constructed a high watch-tower that would let crew members scan the horizon for whales and other surface marine animals.

To devote himself to his dream, Cousteau took a temporary leave from the French Navy. In June 1951, he was at the helm when *Calypso* embarked from Toulon on its first voyage as a research ship. Also along on this trial run, besides

Winches, cables, and diving gear crowd the deck of Cousteau's *Calypso*.

the crew, were Simone Cousteau, the two Cousteau boys, now ages 13 and 11, and a group of wealthy benefactors who had contributed generously to the project.

After this trial run in the Mediterranean, Cousteau and his crew, with scientists aboard, began their first real explorations. On November 24, 1951, *Calypso* sailed to the coral reefs in the Red Sea off the Saudi Arabian coast. While resident scientists used soundings to explore the volcanic origins of undersea basins in the Red Sea, the divers took thousands of photographs and collected samples of underwater species never before studied.

In February 1952, *Calypso* returned to Toulon. For his next project, Cousteau went back to the subject of sunken ships, in part because such projects had a better chance of attracting funding. He anchored *Calypso* near a wreck about 12 miles off Marseilles, France. On his first dive, he retrieved three pottery cups from the wreck. Experts who examined the artifacts determined that the ship was the remains of a Roman vessel sunk in the third century B.C. Cousteau and his divers spent two years exploring the ruins.

At the same time, he was working on a book about his early diving experiences. Written in English with American assistant James Dugan, *The Silent World* was published in the United States in 1953, to critical acclaim. Cousteau later rewrote the book in his native language for publication in France. Eventually, the book was translated into 22 languages.

The Silent World brought Cousteau worldwide attention, which greatly aided him in his perpetual struggle to finance his explorations. Just when a government grant fell through, Cousteau received a proposal that he and his divers conduct offshore explorations for oil in the Persian Gulf off the coast of Abu Dhabi (an emirate, or state, that later became part of the United Arab Emirates).

The British oil company that hired them was convinced that Cousteau and his aqualunged divers could locate potential drilling sites at a lower cost than was possible with traditional methods. And locate oil they did—but it was not easy. The task of drilling proved harder than expected. When several attempts to drill into the hard rock at the bottom failed, Cousteau sent down two men, one with a chisel

When Cousteau's book *The Silent World* was made into a
film in 1956, he came to New York for the U.S. premiere.

Jacques Cousteau

and the other with a large sledgehammer. The work was backbreaking, but in four months, the divers produced 150 samples from the ocean floor, more than enough to convince British Petroleum that drilling would be profitable. Within eight years, the offshore oil fields that Cousteau's team had scouted were producing 40,000 barrels of oil a day, and Abu Dhabi had become wealthy.

The more Cousteau saw of the undersea world, the deeper he wanted to go and the more he wanted to capture on film. He was always looking for people who might help him in his endeavors. In 1953, he traveled to Cambridge, Massachusetts, to visit Dr. Harold Edgerton in his laboratory. Some years earlier, in his quest to capture high-speed activities with a still camera, Edgerton had invented the strobe light. His photos of a drop of milk splashing from a glass and a bullet penetrating a deck of cards had made him world-famous. Now Cousteau wanted to enlist his help in the cause of deep-sea photography.

The inventor and his son, Bill, readily agreed to spend several summers aboard the *Calypso* working on ways to capture the ocean's mysteries on film. The crew called them Papa Flash and Petit ("small") Flash. In the summer of 1954, the Edgertons brought with them a sophisticated camera and a battery-operated flash, which they attached to a trailer that could be towed by the *Calypso*. The camera and flash automatically began taking pictures when they reached the bottom of the sea. However, since no photographer was along to focus the camera, the resulting pictures were less than ideal. They did, however, enable Cousteau to capture on film life on the ocean floor—3,000 feet below the surface.

Also in 1954, Cousteau won a major financial grant from the French government. The government agreed to pay about two-thirds of the yearly operating costs of the *Calypso*. In return, for nine months of the year, *Calypso* would carry French research scientists. *Calypso* thus became the official French oceanographic ship.

Late in 1954 and early in 1955, *Calypso* was given a thorough overhaul; in the meantime, Cousteau worked on the filmmaking equipment with Frédéric Dumas and a promising young cameraman named Louis Malle. In March 1955, the *Calypso* left Marseilles on a 13,800-mile journey through the Red Sea to the Seychelle Islands in the Indian Ocean, and then on to northern Madagascar. Throughout the trip, the divers made hundreds of dives as Cousteau, assisted by Malle, collected footage for a new feature-length film. The film was eventually given the same title as Cousteau's book, *The Silent World*.

The star of the film was a 60-pound grouper that, enticed by food, "danced" with Dumas while the soundtrack played a Viennese waltz. In other scenes, the camera caught the ocean's more violent moods. Once a baby whale got caught in *Calypso*'s propellers. Its trail of blood attracted a group of 30 sharks, which went on a feeding frenzy. Although the sailors were repelled by the violence of the sharks' attack on the dead whale, they kept filming.

The Silent World premiered at the Cannes Film Festival in April 1956 and won the festival's highest award. A year later, it received an Oscar at Hollywood's Academy Award presentations. Cousteau was fast becoming an international celebrity. As a result of his reputation, he was appointed the director of Monaco's Oceanographic Institute, a marine museum and research organization built in 1899.

As of 1957, Cousteau had been in the French Navy for 27 years. He held the lowest rank of any of the officers in his graduating class, however—a reflection not of Cousteau's ability, but of his interest in his own projects, rather than in being a naval officer. With more and more projects and fund-raising activities consuming his attention, Cousteau realized that it was time to cut the ties. He now resigned from the navy to devote full time to his many projects.

To the Depths

Cousteau and his divers had learned that there were limits to how deep a diver could go, even with the aqualung. Still, Cousteau was not willing to accept those limits as the boundaries to his knowledge about the sea. His work with Harold and Bill Edgerton had convinced him that there were other ways of exploring the sea's depths. In the late 1950s, Harold Edgerton brought Cousteau new equipment to help him explore the Romanche Trench, almost 5 miles below the surface of the Atlantic Ocean. To withstand the enormous pressure of such a depth, Edgerton housed a camera in a tempered stainless-steel case that could withstand 5.5 tons of pressure per square inch.

Edgerton also created a transducer (a device that transmits energy from one system to another) that would signal when the camera got close to the ocean floor. It allowed the camera to focus about 9 feet above the floor. Unfortunately, however, the transducer malfunctioned, and the camera captured only two clear photos. One showed four white creatures; the other revealed a starfish. What were the white creatures, and what did a starfish eat 25,000 feet down?

Frustrated with robot oceanography, Cousteau wanted to see the depths himself. He was not the only person who

As director of Monaco's Oceanographic Institute, Cousteau
showed Prince Rainier and Princess Grace a new exhibit.

Jacques Cousteau

wanted to go to the ocean floor. Auguste Piccard continued to work on underwater vehicles, and Cousteau had been involved with later versions of Piccard's bathyscaphe. Cousteau, however, was beginning to feel that such vehicles were too large and unwieldy for his purposes.

He turned his inventive mind to alternatives. For six years, he and two engineers worked on building a smaller, more easily maneuvered undersea vehicle. Shaped like a turtle, Hull No. 1 stood 5 feet tall and had two windows, a top hatch, lights, and viewing ports. It was designed to descend to a depth of 1,150 feet and stay below for at least three hours. Instead of cumbersome propellers, this small submarine was thrust forward by a series of jet nozzles. The pilot simply swiveled the nozzles to change direction or control speed. As a result, the sub could maneuver underwater almost as easily as an individual diver could. Cousteau equipped the small submarine with a mechanical claw, to scoop up samples of underwater plant-and-animal life, and cameras, to record the sights.

In March 1958, Cousteau launched the unmanned vehicle in the Mediterranean for a test run. Pushing the limits of its design, Hull No. 1 descended to 2,000 feet without a problem. While the crew tried to hoist the vehicle aboard the *Calypso* after the test, however, a cable snapped. The precious vehicle dropped 3,300 feet to the bottom, too deep to be retrieved.

Cousteau spent another 18 months building Hull No 2. When it was finished, the crew thought it looked like a comic-book version of a flying saucer. So Cousteau named it the Diving Saucer, or DS-2. The vessel was first launched on October 9, 1959, in the Caribbean Sea, off the coast of Puerto Rico. During the first experiments, the saucer performed well. Several days later, however, when two divers were

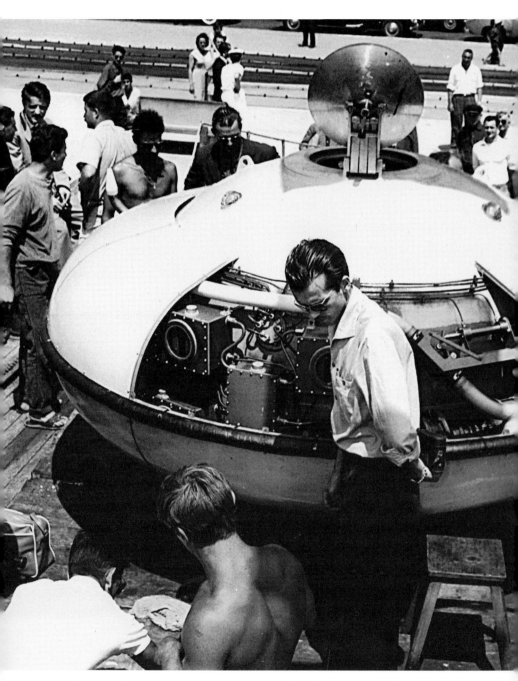

Cousteau's Diving Saucer was designed to dive to 1,000 feet.

Jacques Cousteau

surfacing in the saucer from a 230-foot dive, the copper battery compartment short-circuited, causing an explosion. Sailors quickly submerged the vehicle, to extinguish the flames. After repairing the damage, the technicians switched to lead power packs for batteries, which also failed. Another trial ended when water leaked inside the interior batteries, causing them to burst inward, starting a fire.

Cousteau was nevertheless determined to make the saucer work. In February 1960, after more trial-and-error, he and a companion took the saucer down to 1,000 feet, and it worked perfectly. On this trip, Cousteau saw "gray blobs." He did not know what they were, but he was convinced they were the first humans to see such creatures alive.

Since its first successful dive, DS-2 has made more than 1,070 dives around the world. In order to free *Calypso* from the job of transporting the diving saucer, Cousteau and his technicians designed the world's largest inflatable ship. Deflated, it can be flown anywhere in the world and then inflated and launched.

LIVING UNDERWATER

DS-2 allowed Cousteau and his divers to go deeper than they ever had before, but Cousteau also wanted to be able to stay longer underwater. The main problem with a diver staying longer was nitrogen saturation of human tissues, which caused the bends when divers surfaced.

In the 1950s, George Bond, a U.S. Navy diving expert, suggested that once the body's tissues were saturated with nitrogen, it did not matter how much longer a diver stayed underwater. Whether several hours, a week, or a month, a

In 1961, Cousteau was presented the Hubbard Medal for distinction in exploration, discovery, and research by U.S. President John F. Kennedy.

diver would still have to take the same amount of decompression time. Therefore, reasoned Bond, wouldn't it make more sense for divers to stay underwater for days at a time? Cousteau—and others—quickly set out to find a way.

Jacques Cousteau

On September 14, 1962, Cousteau launched Continental Shelf Station No 1 (Conshelf I) near Marseilles. It was the first inhabited structure on the ocean floor. Conshelf I was 17 feet long and 8 feet high. The station housed two divers—Albert Falco and Claude Wesly—35 feet underwater for one week. Although the living quarters were small, the divers enjoyed many of the comforts of home. Hot water for showers was piped down through a plastic tube from the ship, and gourmet meals were sent down in pressure cookers.

How would humans respond to staying underwater for days at a time? As it turned out, the endurance required of the divers was more psychological than physical. At first, Falco experienced horrible nightmares in which he felt as if he were being strangled. He became irritable and complained bitterly about the telephone calls from the surface, which interrupted his experiments. He also complained of the divers from the surface, who stirred up the silt around the station. When Cousteau gave orders to cut down on the number of telephone calls and told the surface divers to avoid the station, Falco's mood improved. By the end of the week, he admitted that he had enjoyed the week underwater, because for the first time in 20 years of diving, he had had enough time to truly observe his underwater environment.

While living in Conshelf I, Falco and Wesly worked in the open water for up to five hours a day, going to depths of 85 feet. Their experiment proved that humans could live and work underwater for extended periods of time. To keep two men underwater for a week, however, required the constant support of scores of people on the surface.

The success of Conshelf I convinced Cousteau that his dream that humans would colonize the sea, living and working on the ocean floor, was possible. Immediately, he devised an even larger project: Conshelf II. Five "oceanauts," as Cousteau called them, would live 33 feet below the surface for a month. And for one week of that time, two others—experienced diving instructors—would live and work at another station 85 feet down. Cousteau, as the leader of the entire project, could not take on the job of oceanaut. He had to be free to be either underwater or aboard ship, as circumstances required.

To prove that he could manage this type of project beyond his home waters of the Mediterranean, Jacques Cousteau chose a location in the Red Sea: the Roman Reef, a coral reef off the coast of Sudan. The size of the project required two support ships—the *Calypso* and a chartered freighter, the *Rosaldo*. Besides delivering the prefabricated underwater station, *Rosaldo* served as power supply and storage depot, and as headquarters for the 54 scientists, technicians, cameramen, and divers who would support the oceanauts. *Calypso* was subsequently left free to make periodic trips to Port Sudan for fresh supplies.

Conshelf II consisted of four main buildings and eight smaller structures. The air-conditioned headquarters in Conshelf II was Starfish House, named for its shape. This building was where the oceanauts lived and worked. Besides providing sleeping space for eight, it contained a kitchen, dining area, laboratory, and photography room. On the same level were two other main buildings: a wet garage for underwater scooters and tools and a domed hangar for DS-2. The fourth main building—the only structure at 85 feet—called Deep Cabin, was where the two deep divers would live for a week. The smaller structures were pens for keeping fish that the divers captured and antishark cages posted around the edges of the colony.

Cousteau speaks with divers on Conshelf III, which followed Conshelf II. The Conshelf experiments were the first to study the effects on humans of living underwater for long periods.

Cousteau and his team had planned Conshelf II carefully. Still, there were setbacks. Divers checking on Starfish House shortly before the oceanauts were due to descend found it filled with a thick fog. Technicians finally figured out that the air compressor on the *Rosaldo*, unaccustomed to the intense heat and humidity of the area, was sending down tiny beads of water covered with an oily film. Cousteau sent an engineer to France to get the right kind of filters to cope with the problem.

BELLS TO BATHYSCAPHES

According to the theory of evolution, life began in the water. Only much later did some forms of life crawl onto the land and adapt to breathing air. Perhaps this ancient connection with water explains the fascination that some humans have long had with the idea of living underwater.

Legend has it that the great warrior Alexander the Great (356–323 B.C.) had himself lowered into the sea in a glass barrel big enough to hold one person. He claimed that while underwater he saw a fish so large that it took three days to swim past the barrel!

Much later, in 1538, two Greek inventors built an open-bottom diving bell and demonstrated it in the Tagus River near Toledo, Spain. Open-bottom diving bells work on the principle that water will enter the open end only to the point where the water pressure is equal to the pressure of the air within the chamber. Depending on the depth to which the bell is lowered, that could be a few inches or a few feet. Enterprising folks soon put the diving bell to practical use, salvaging treasure and cannons from sunken ships, working on underwater sections of lighthouses and bridges, and repairing ships' hulls.

Sir Edmund Halley, discoverer of Halley's comet, which he predicted would appear in 1682, built an improved diving bell. In his ingenious method, stale air was replaced with fresh air through a leather tube from the surface. Halley himself went down to 60 feet in such a bell and stayed for an hour and a half. His bell was later used for salvage work.

Ideas for self-propelled underwater vehicles go back to the sixteenth century. The first working model was built in 1620 by Cornelis Drebbel, a Dutch scientist living in England. Drebbel covered a wooden boat with leather and then coated the whole thing with grease. Six passengers could be rowed by 12 oarsmen working oars that were also encased in leather to make the boat watertight. Drebbel sailed his submarine several times in the Thames River.

During the American Revolution, David Bushnell of Connecticut built a one-man underwater combat vehicle. On the night he was to use the vessel against the British, Bushnell got sick. Someone took his

place, and Bushnell's submarine was sent out to attach explosives to a British warship. The warship's wooden hull was covered with copper, however, and the screws provided to attach the explosives to the ship could not penetrate it. Nevertheless, when the British discovered the vessel and pursued it, the man in Bushnell's submarine hurled the explosives at them and scared them off.

The most famous undersea vessel of the nineteenth century was fictitious. In his novel *Twenty Thousand Leagues Under the Sea* (published in 1862), Jules Verne described a submarine, called the *Nautilus*. Verne, who based his fiction on the most current scientific thought and experimentation, imagined the *Nautilus* to be powered by an electric motor. Sure enough, electric power played an extremely important part in the design of the first practical submarines, which appeared in the early 1900s. These submarines were used very effectively in combat during World War I.

An illustration from a thirteenth-century manuscript shows how Alexander the Great supposedly lowered himself undersea in a glass barrel.

The first person to have success using an underwater vehicle to conduct scientific research was Dr. William Beebe, an American naturalist. Between 1931 and 1934, Beebe dived to depths of more than 3,000 feet in a bathysphere (deep sphere). In 1948, Dr. Auguste Piccard continued to make strides where Beebe had left off and designed a bathyscaphe (deep ship). He tested his bathyscaphe with the expert help of Jacques Cousteau.

There were other difficulties with Deep Cabin. Twice, as it was being readied for occupation, the three-story cylinder broke loose from its moorings and rolled down the reef. The second time this happened, an electrician was trapped inside. It took hours of work to rescue the electrician and find a way to secure the cabin against further wanderings.

In spite of the setbacks, Conshelf II was a success. The oceanauts reveled in the calm surroundings as they played chess and watched schools of fish swim by the windows of Starfish House. A doctor visited every day to check their health and found no problems—although he did note that the increased atmospheric pressure caused beards to grow much more slowly than at the surface.

Life up above was not so pleasant or healthful. The project had been planned for March, when the temperatures in the Red Sea would have been bearable. Delays had pushed the start back four months, to July. Temperatures were now in the 90s and above, with a humidity level around 100 percent. These conditions and the hard work needed to keep everything running smoothly drained the energy of the above-water-surface crew. Cousteau himself lost 20 pounds during that month.

One day, Simone Cousteau could stand the heat no longer. She donned an aqualung and descended to the air-conditioned comfort of Starfish House, where she remained for the duration of the project, thus becoming the first female oceanaut. A few days later, she and Jacques celebrated their 26th wedding anniversary with a party in Starfish House.

As Cousteau had hoped, Conshelf II proved that humans could live in the sea for extended periods of time. Even the divers in Deep Cabin fared well. Breathing an atmosphere of mixed air and helium, they had been able to work at depths

Simone Cousteau accompanied her husband on
many of his sea voyages during their long marriage.

Cousteau's son Philippe, shown here with his
mother, was one of the oceanauts on Conshelf III.

of 165 feet and make brief dives as deep as 363 feet without
experiencing nitrogen narcosis.

Conshelf II, like almost all of Cousteau's projects, was also
the subject of a film. *World Without Sun* won a second
Academy Award for Cousteau. But Cousteau still had to
struggle to get funding for his projects. Underwater exploration now had to compete with space programs for money
and public attention. Also, other people were beginning to

establish their own undersea stations on the continental shelf. Shortly after Conshelf II, George Bond, one of the earliest supporters of underwater living, established Sealab I, an underwater station, for the U.S. Navy. On Sealab I, four divers spent 11 days 193 feet below the ocean's surface.

Cousteau, responding to the challenge to go deeper, began planning Conshelf III. In September 1965, six divers went down to a depth of 325 feet to live and work for 21 days. One of the divers was Cousteau's 24-year-old son Philippe. Unlike the two previous Conshelf projects, this one was too deep for surface divers to visit safely; the oceanauts were on their own for three weeks. Still, the project was a success. Like the other Conshelf experiments, it showed that divers could perform useful work at great depths.

Cousteau hoped that oil executives and other industrialists would see the value of undersea research stations and that the Conshelf experiments would result in lucrative contracts for his organization. Unfortunately, while industrialists saw the value of Cousteau's work and were willing to use his group for some jobs, they mostly turned to less expensive ways of working on the ocean floor, such as with robots and small submarines. It seemed that big business was unwilling to accept Cousteau's challenge to colonize the deep.

While this door was closing for Cousteau, however, another was opening. It would make his name a household word around the globe.

CHAPTER FIVE

A

WORLDWIDE

AUDIENCE

As with all his projects, Cousteau produced a film of the Conshelf III experiment. This time, however, despite the success of his two previous Academy Award-winning films, movie theaters were not interested in showing the film. Perhaps the title—*Experience Précontinent III*—lacked the drama of his other titles, or perhaps they felt that moviegoers had seen enough underwater adventures. Whatever the reason, Cousteau was left with reels of film and no audience.

At the time, the National Geographic Society was beginning to produce a series of television specials on nature. Cousteau offered his film to the society, which accepted, with one condition: It wanted Hollywood producer David

Cousteau stands in his diving gear during the Conshelf experiment.

ANATOMY OF A COUSTEAU TELEVISION SHOW

Jacques Cousteau and his crews had to maintain a tight schedule to produce four hours of television a year, especially with such unpredictable subjects as sea creatures. There usually were two crews working in two different parts of the world—one on *Calypso*, and one on a ship leased for the occasion.

The Captain, as Cousteau was called, was often away from the film locations managing the Cousteau Group—16 interconnected organizations devoted to such activities as oceanographic research, marine engineering, the manufacturing of diving equipment, and filmmaking. In addition, he was still director of the Oceanographic Institute in Monaco. Thus, he would often arrive at the filming location for a few days, be photographed with the animals, and then return to his other duties.

Long before the filming began, however, ideas for shows were gathered from many sources: Cousteau, his sons, the divers, TV executives, and so on. A research team read whatever information they could find on the chosen topics. Writers then developed story lines. Once on location, the camera operators did their best to capture on film what the writers had specified. At the same time, the camera crew filmed whatever unexpected but interesting events occurred.

A day's filming began with a group meeting to decide what shots were needed and who would do what. If Jacques Cousteau was aboard, he approved the general shooting plan. Then, his son Philippe or another second-in-command made the specific work assignments. Once the divers were in the water, Jacques directed their activity from the ship by means of closed-circuit television and radiophones in the divers' helmets. As he watched, Cousteau might jot down what he saw the divers filming. After a 45-minute dive, the divers would surface, and Cousteau would interview them about what they had seen while the events were fresh in their minds.

This description sounds very efficient, but in reality, events were completely dependent on the whims of the weather and the animals. Film crews might wait three months in a location for the right weather and animals and then get everything they needed in one 24-hour period. On average, ten dives yielded one sequence of usable film.

Some animals presented more difficulties than others. Whales and dolphins were especially tricky to film. The only way to get a shot of a whale was to try to get ahead of it and slow it down. During the first summer of shooting, camera operators tried everything. They would chase a whale in one of their small inflatable motorboats, jump into the water in front of the whale, wait a minute or so for their masks to defog, and then start filming. But the whale would quickly disappear into the distance. Even when divers managed to climb on top of a whale and hold onto a fin, the whale would speed off. Often, the developed film would show only the tail of the departing whale.

Still, Cousteau's divers were persistent. They always managed to get enough usable film. For one show, they might shoot up to 140,000 feet of film. Back in California, film editors would reduce that to 2,000 feet for a one-hour telecast. Then, an editor would write the final narration. Although he was not involved in the editing process, Cousteau always saw the final version and gave his approval.

It was a cumbersome process, but a rewarding one. Jacques Cousteau's television specials have won 11 Emmy Awards.

Cousteau talks with his divers, who sit behind one of the submersibles.

Wolper to oversee the editing of the film. Cousteau agreed. In May 1966, American television viewers got their first taste of Cousteau's underwater explorations, on the hour-long *World of Jacques Cousteau*.

The people at David Wolper Productions had been so impressed with Cousteau's filmmaking ability that they urged him to do more television specials. To make that commitment, though, Cousteau needed to know that he would have the necessary financial backing. In the late 1960s, he took his proposal for a TV series to all three major American television networks. ABC made the best offer. The network would finance 12 hour-long shows, to be televised over a period of three years. Cousteau's film company, Sharks Associated, would do the filming, and David Wolper Productions would do the editing and postproduction work. Besides getting funding from ABC, Cousteau also kept the right to sell the films in Europe, Africa, and Asia.

Cousteau finally had the financial backing he needed to make long-range plans. For the series, *Calypso* would travel to all the world's oceans, filming whatever Cousteau and his divers found of interest. There was a price to pay, though: Cousteau's emphasis would no longer be on underwater research, but on seeking out the most dramatic scenes for television audiences.

To make his divers look more glamorous for TV, Cousteau outfitted them with new, more photogenic equipment—hydrodynamic (the water equivalent of aerodynamic) air tanks, shimmering black diving suits with yellow stripes down the arms and body, and bright yellow helmets with built-in lights and radiotelephones. *Calypso* too underwent dramatic changes. Research labs were turned into photographic darkrooms; the old observation chamber was

Jacques Cousteau encounters a school
of fish while diving in the Indian Ocean.

replaced with a new, larger one; and a closed-circuit television system was installed.

To propel them underwater, the divers were given new underwater scooters with lights and cameras mounted on them. For surface travel, Cousteau acquired small inflatable boats with outboard motors, called zodiacs. To organize the miles of film he intended to take, Cousteau came up with two new ideas. The first was to have divers describe what they were filming over the radiotelephone in their helmets to a tape recorder on the ship. The density of the air the divers had to breathe, however, turned their voices into cartoonlike gibberish. Cousteau's other idea was a computer that would code film sequences according to subject matter, thus making any image readily available to the film editors. However, the computer programming never worked properly. Thus, both concepts were unsuccessful.

In February 1967, the remodeled *Calypso* left Monaco on its new mission: to capture for American TV audiences the drama of undersea life. The mission was wildly successful. The first episode of *The Undersea World of Jacques Cousteau*, called "Sharks," received critical acclaim for its blending of education and entertainment. For the first time in Cousteau's filmmaking career, however, some criticized his approach. Negative attention focused on his emphasis of the dramatic rather than scientific research. Shark specialist Eugenie Clark, who had been aboard the *Calypso* for some of the shooting, was one of the critics. She pointed out that the need to keep producing film footage sometimes got in the way of scientific purity.

Cousteau replied to these criticisms by saying that his aim in the television series was to give people rare glimpses of nature that they could not experience on their own. He saw

"Mysteries of the Hidden Reefs," part of *The Undersea World of Jacques Cousteau* series, examined coral and the environmental threats it was facing.

himself and his camera operators as observers, not scientists, and his shows as adventures rather than documentaries.

To capture the sense of adventure that he and his crew experienced, Cousteau made sure that each of the TV segments told a story. He wanted viewers to become involved by wondering what would happen next. To make the films more personal, he made the divers and crew part of that story. So "Sharks," for example, was not just the story of sharks but also of how Cousteau and his team captured the story of the sharks on film.

Cousteau also recognized the importance of humor in keeping viewers involved. In one episode filmed in Africa, in order to get close to a group of hippopotamuses, two cameramen disguised themselves in a life-size hippopotamus outfit. The final film shows not only the majestic hippos but also the two cameramen staggering out of the water in their hilarious costume.

Family Matters

Cousteau's two sons—now grown men—were both involved in the Cousteau business. Jean-Michel, who had studied architecture, took on the unexciting but vital role of behind-the-scenes administrator. He was the organizer, the planner, and the procurer of supplies for *Calypso*. Eventually, feeling unappreciated by his father, he struck out on his own, occasionally taking jobs as a marine architect, lecturing about diving and marine life, and taking wealthy vacationers on diving tours around the world.

Philippe, on the other hand, had a creative role in the Cousteau organization. In school, he had planned to get a degree in engineering, but at the last minute, he switched to filmmaking. Philippe played a key part in the filming of many episodes of *The Undersea World of Jacques Cousteau*, as either photographer, director, or star diver. But there was always a certain amount of tension between Philippe and his father.

During the planning stages of the series, Philippe had fallen in love with an American model, Janice Sullivan. After a courtship that spanned two continents, Janice and Philippe decided to marry. Jacques and Simone Cousteau objected strenuously—a model was not good enough for their son, and an American model who could not speak French was out of the question. They demanded that Philippe call off the wedding. He refused, and he and Janice were married in Paris in January 1967. Jacques and Simone did not attend. Their sole wedding gift was French-language lessons for Janice.

Despite his displeasure at the marriage, Jacques Cousteau continued to work with Philippe on the TV series. To produce four segments a year, father and son were both needed to oversee the filmmaking crews, come up with new topics,

Philippe Cousteau was nominated for an Emmy Award in the news and documentary category for his underwater camera work on "The Singing Whale" episode of *The Undersea World of Jacques Cousteau.*

find the best locations for shooting, and develop new technologies to cope with unique filming problems.

Philippe attempted to reduce the tension by putting distance between himself and his father. He and Janice moved to California, where they could be near the film editors. At the same time, Jacques Cousteau approved Philippe's plan to take up hot-air ballooning, which Philippe believed would add a new dimension to the Cousteau filming capabilities. The hot-air balloon was useful in many ways—for photographing from above and for scouting passages for *Calypso* among reefs and atolls. In 1968, Jacques authorized Philippe to lease a ship in California and help produce a television segment on the gray whale (this segment later appeared as part of the Cousteau series). By 1969, however, Philippe felt the need to separate from his father. He began his own production company, Thalassa Films.

THE ENVIRONMENTALIST

In his early days of underwater exploration and discovery, Cousteau paid little attention to the harmful effect that humans could have on the ocean and its creatures. In 1948, in one of his first encounters with whales, Cousteau harpooned a pilot whale in the Atlantic Ocean merely to dissect it and discover what it fed on. Over the next 25 years, though, he had become increasingly concerned about the environment.

The early 1970s were a time when many people were beginning to share that concern. In 1974, Cousteau launched a new nonprofit organization, the Cousteau Society, with headquarters in the United States, to work for the preservation of the world's oceans.

For one episode of *The Undersea World of Jacques Cousteau*, divers visited an otter in a kelp bed.

About the same time, Jacques began to realize how much he missed Philippe's enthusiasm and creative ideas. In time, father and son began to work together more closely. Their reconciliation was complete in 1976, when Janice Cousteau gave birth to the couple's first child. In the same year, Philippe became director of his father's film production company and vice-president of the Cousteau Society.

Although 1976 was a good year for family relations, it was a difficult one for the Cousteau business. *The Undersea World of Jacques Cousteau* had been enormously popular for several years, and the ABC television network had twice renewed the three-year contract, but now the show was beginning to lose its audience. ABC announced that the May 1976 segment would be the last.

Cousteau was now losing not only the outlet for his creative work but also the money that kept *Calypso* and all his other projects going. To support his many costly trips, Cousteau had to produce—and sell—four films a year. Cousteau had always been skilled in selling his projects, however, and soon he had convinced the Atlantic-Richfield oil company to give public television station KCET a grant to produce 12 Cousteau films. *The Cousteau Odyssey* series took Cousteau in a new direction. Unlike the exhilarating action-adventure stories of his previous series, this one focused on problems—environmental calamities, vanishing civilizations, human tragedies. For example, in Alaska, it covered the clash of natives, industrialists, and environmentalists over natural resources; in Cuba and Haiti, it compared different approaches to environmental management.

The *Cousteau Odyssey* series explored topics on land as well as undersea. Here, Cousteau visits Easter Island, off the coast of Chile.

By the time that the *Odyssey* series was filmed, great advances had been made in underwater camera equipment.

In the midst of filming this TV series, Cousteau and his family experienced their own personal tragedy. Philippe Cousteau's true love was flying. As a result of his enthusiasm, *Calypso* now carried a seaplane, a hot-air balloon, and a hang glider. Philippe enjoyed piloting all of them, but especially the seaplane, the *Flying Calypso*, from which he could shoot aerial photographs. In June 1979, the *Flying Calypso* was undergoing repairs in Portugal. Philippe flew there to test the repaired plane. After a test run, he began to land the plane on the Tagus River. The landing was normal—a thud as the plane hit the water, and then a few skips as it slowed down. Suddenly, the plane rolled over and ripped apart. Philippe was killed instantly. A few days later, he was buried at sea.

Cousteau mourned his son deeply, and for a while he found it hard to take an interest in his work. His family finally convinced him to put aside his grief and move on. Jean-Michel decided to return to the family business and took charge of the Cousteau Society.

When his contract with the Public Broadcasting System ended, Cousteau had to go looking for financial support once again. He found both money and a kindred spirit in Ted Turner, the owner of a cable TV network and a committed environmentalist. As a child, he was inspired by

Portuguese Navy divers carry Philippe
Cousteau's body away from the Tagus River.

Jacques Cousteau

Jean-Michel and Jacques Cousteau wade
in the Amazon River near the *Calypso*.

Cousteau's films and books. He agreed to support an ambitious Cousteau undertaking—the exploration of the world's second-longest river, the Amazon in South America. The resulting films would be broadcast over the Turner cable network.

The Amazon expedition began in February 1982. Over the course of two years, 48 crew members traveled 4,000 miles exploring the river from the water, the land, and the air. Thirty-five scientists joined the expedition at various points.

To cover the vast territory, sometimes four different film teams were at work in several different countries. During the course of the expedition, crews were in Peru, Brazil, Colombia, Bolivia, and a few other Amazon countries. As the expedition got underway, a land crew, led by Jean-Michel, started at the Amazon's source high in the Peruvian Andes and traced the river as it flowed east. At the same time, *Calypso* sailed west up the river from its mouth in the Atlantic. When the ship could go no farther, it turned around and came back down the river, exploring some of the Amazon's tributaries.

The first three shows produced from the Amazon expedition focused on the river, its animals, and its people. The last one took Cousteau in a new direction. At the urging of Jean-Michel, who believed that human activity had a significant effect on the river, Cousteau devoted the hour-long show to the illegal drug traffic in the Amazon region. With this film, Jacques Cousteau moved toward becoming a commentator on the general ills of society.

Although much of his time now was taken up with organizing and fund raising, Cousteau continued to develop ideas for new inventions. As usual, he sought help whenever he needed it. Working with Jacques Constans, a staff member, he designed a device to analyze the surface layer of water. They named it the Sea Spider, because of its many spindly arms.

In the early 1980s, Cousteau also devoted much thought to developing a way to reduce oil consumption by ships. The result was the Turbosail™ a device that uses wind power to propel a ship. The ship is not solely dependent on the wind, however. Its diesel engines are programmed to maintain the desired speed regardless of wind conditions.

Even so, the Turbosail™ reduces a ship's oil consumption by about 40 percent.

As with his most famous invention, the aqualung, Jacques Cousteau experienced several setbacks with the Turbosail™. As it turned out, the problems were caused by the design of the ship on which the Turbosail™ was mounted. When that was corrected, the Turbosail™ worked fine. The *Alcyone,* Cousteau's "windship," made its first successful sail in May 1985.

In the same year, after celebrating his 75th birthday in June, Cousteau launched a five-year expedition that would take film crews aboard *Calypso* and *Alcyone* around the world and produce many television specials. Called *Rediscovery of the World,* the series focused not only on the environment but also on the place of human beings within the environment.

The *Alcyone* has two Turbosails™, which rise from the boat's deck.

For this expedition, Cousteau gave his team a new look and new equipment. He wanted both to increase efficiency by making use of new technologies and to give the divers a high-technology image for the new TV series. Engineers tried out a variety of materials to create a stronger and lighter tank for compressed air. A new helmet design included built-in headphones. Microphones were included in the mouthpieces so that divers could talk to one another and to the crew on the surface. New underwater scooters had built-in air tanks and regulators so that divers did not have to waste time strapping on their tanks. The new suits, helmets, gloves, masks, fins, and scooters were all silver with black stripes, to increase lighting in dark areas of the ocean and to give the divers a space-age look. Perhaps the biggest change of all was in the filming. After using a movie camera for 62 years, Jacques Cousteau now turned to the new medium of video, which gives the filmmaker more flexibility and considerably reduces the expense.

In the summer of 1985, the Cousteau crews began their five-year expedition in Haiti, examining the social upheaval in that Caribbean island. From there, *Calypso* went on to the nearby Communist nation of Cuba, where Cousteau interviewed Fidel Castro and was instrumental in obtaining the release of 50 political prisoners. After the Cuba filming, *Calypso* traveled to Miami, Florida, for repairs. Meanwhile, *Alcyone* went around the southern tip of South America and up the west coast of the Americas, stopping along the way to film. In June 1987, the windship made a three-month tour around the Bering Sea. After that, *Alcyone* took its turn in dry dock for maintenance.

In the meantime, workers had completed extensive repairs on *Calypso*. In June 1986, the ship passed through the

While most of his divers wore their new silver suits in 1985, Cousteau stuck to the yellow-and-black outfit.

Panama Canal and sailed toward the South Pacific, New Zealand, and Australia. In May 1988, the two Cousteau ships met up in Papua New Guinea. Later that year, *Calypso* filmed in Borneo, while the crew of *Alcyone* studied the ecology of Eniwetok Island, 30 years after it had been the site of a series of atomic bomb tests. Later filming occurred in Indonesia and Vietnam.

Cousteau had planned to finish up *Rediscovery of the World* with a study of the Yangtze River in China. But he had difficulty obtaining the necessary permission and papers, so the project was postponed.

Since the completion of *Rediscovery of the World*, Cousteau has continued to make films and to promote environmental concerns through the Cousteau Society. In 1992, he presented a new film at the worldwide Earth Summit in Rio de Janeiro, Brazil, and appealed to world leaders to protect the environment.

THE
COUSTEAU
LEGACY

While he has never claimed to be a scientist, Jacques Cousteau did perfect the science of underwater exploration. Before him, those who wanted to experience the underwater environment firsthand had to do so locked into awkward diving suits and bound to the surface by air hoses. After Cousteau and Émile Gagnan invented the aqualung, divers were freed to move about underwater as naturally as they moved on land. They were not limited by the length of an air hose, nor did they have to remain upright. They could swim with, and like, the fishes. This freedom opened up a vast new world of possibilities for underwater research, work, and recreation.

Divers attach special equipment to *Deepstar 4000*, a three-person research submarine capable of diving 4,000 feet.

Jacques Cousteau

In 1946, just a year after the end of World War II, Air Liquide, the French company that employed Émile Gagnan, produced the first commercial aqualung. By 1950, only ten had been exported to the United States. When U.S. distributors were asked how many more they wanted to order, the answer was, "None." The market was saturated, they claimed. They could not have been more wrong. Ten years later—long before his television shows made Jacques Cousteau's name a household word in the United States— *Time* magazine estimated that a million American skin divers enjoyed the benefits of the aqualung. Today, millions of divers all over the world use the aqualung for work and for recreation.

In the 50-plus years since Cousteau and Gagnan invented the aqualung, many engineers have tinkered with the design, attempting to improve upon it. Every improvement, however, has been based upon the basic principle of the original Cousteau-Gagnan design.

The main change in the aqualung has been a switch to a single-hose rather than a double-hose regulator. Between 1957 and 1961, engineers sought a way to make the aqualung lighter and smaller, and thus easier for women to use. The result was the single-hose regulator, which is not only more compact and more comfortable but is also easier to breathe through. By the mid-1960s, the single-hose regulator had become very popular. Today, only one manufacturer markets a double-hose regulator.

Cousteau divers, though, continue to use their old double-hose regulators, for a number of reasons. For one thing, the double-hose regulator releases air bubbles at the back of the diver's head, thus allowing camera operators to see their subjects more easily. Because the old regulators are made of

Over the course of his long career, Cousteau wrote some 20 books and made more than 90 films and television documentaries.

heavier material, they are sturdier. They are also less com-plicated and thus need less maintenance. Finally, Cousteau divers prefer the more difficult breathability of the old dou-ble-hose regulators, because they let the diver feel changes in the air supply. Instead of relying on reading gauges, the diver gets a physical reminder of the diminishing supply of air in his or her tanks.

In the years since the invention of the aqualung, an entire industry has been developed to serve the needs of divers. The modern diver has a host of aids available: wet suits, div-ing suits that allow a small amount of water between the skin and suit, which provides some warmth; dry suits for use in frigid waters; buoyancy compensators, which allow divers to float weightless at any depth; depth gauges to use to figure out diving tables and decompression limits; and dive computers, which track dives and calculate decom-pression and depth limits. Yet Jean-Michel Cousteau warns against relying too much on machines. Modern divers may use diving computers instead of diving tables. Yet comput-ers can malfunction. With the older, simpler equipment, divers had to think more for themselves, and this had its advantages.

Although the aqualung changed the course of diving his-tory, it also taught Jacques Cousteau and others that scuba divers could only go so deep (during Conshelf II, two divers breathing a combination of air and helium reached 363 feet safely without experiencing nitrogen narcosis). For deeper dives, other kinds of equipment were needed. In this field, Jacques Cousteau and his diving teams also led the way. Cousteau's other major underwater innovations—the sub-mersible (DS-2) and the manned underwater Conshelf stations—were followed by a host of similar underwater exploration aids, which divers are still using to investigate the ocean depths.

In 1979, Sylvia Earle, wearing an armored suit equipped with a self-contained air supply, became the first person to explore the ocean floor at 1,250 feet. In 1988, during an experiment called the Hydra VIII, a team of six divers set another record by living and working for six days 1,706 feet below the surface of the ocean off Marseilles, France. During their stay, the divers breathed a synthetic mixture, which contained a high percentage of hydrogen. Today, divers in submersibles regularly explore some of the deepest parts of the world's oceans. In the late 1990s, Graham Hawkes, inventor and pilot of the submersible Deep Flight—which looks more like a jet plane than a traditional submersible— hopes to "fly" 7 miles down into the Mariana Trench, the

Sylvia Earle, chief scientist at the National Oceanic and Atmospheric Administration, is one of many modern divers to benefit from advances made by Cousteau.

deepest point on Earth. Deep Flight, unlike typical research vehicles, is made of a super-strong material that will allow it to withstand the pressures found at such a depth.

ENVIRONMENTAL CONCERNS TODAY

Neither Jacques Cousteau nor his divers have focused on discovering new underwater species, cataloging the ocean's resources, or mapping its depths. Instead, their contribution to our knowledge of the deep has been twofold. First, they led the way underwater so that others could conduct their research safely and efficiently. Second, through their films, they continue to make the public aware of the incredible beauty of the ocean and the numerous dangers to it from thoughtless human usage.

Cousteau is still a visible leader in the movement to take care of the ocean, but his concern for the environment is broader than that. Several years ago, he saw that the fight to save the ocean and its creatures had to be connected to the fight to save the whole planet. In 1991, he launched a campaign to obtain 20 million signatures from people around the world on a petition entitled "The Rights of Future Generations." By mid-1995, some 9 million people had signed the petition.

COUSTEAU TODAY

Jacques Cousteau has had a lifelong love affair with the water. Early on, his love spawned curiosity, and this curiosity led to exploration. From the beginning, his motto, repeated often to his divers, has been *Il faut aller voir* ("We must go see for ourselves").

Cousteau's determination to see for himself forced him into the role of inventor. Two qualities have made him so successful in that role: an appreciation for the work of those who came before him—both their successes and their failures—and a commitment to teamwork. Cousteau has always realized when his ideas needed the expertise of a specialist to carry them out. With each of his innovations, he has sought the technical help he needed.

Cousteau is deeply serious about his work and the various causes to which he is committed, but that has not kept him from enjoying his life. To Cousteau, having fun is an important part of life. In fact, he sees work and play as interchangeable. He says that he was playing when he invented the aqualung. He is still playing today. He continues to dive, though now only in warm water. After all, age deserves some compromises.

In December 1990, Simone Cousteau died at the age of 72. Two years later, Cousteau married Francine Triplet, a woman who dives recreationally. They live in Paris.

On June 11, 1995, Jacques-Yves Cousteau turned 85. For some, that might have meant it was time to look back and reflect upon the past. But not for Cousteau. He prefers to look ahead, to plan for the future, and to consider what needs to be done rather than what has already been done.

In an interview around the time of his 85th birthday, Cousteau outlined his two big projects. The first was the work on "The Rights of Future Generations" petition. The second was a replacement for the venerable *Calypso*. The old minesweeper had served Cousteau well but was growing old. Cousteau wanted to replace it with a state-of-the-art

At 85, Cousteau was still busy working to protect the oceans he loves.

oceanographic research ship, using up-to-the-minute technology. According to Cousteau, *Calypso II's* new design allows him to open up the ship to women and children passengers. Crew quarters on the old *Calypso* were too limited to allow separate cabins for men and women.

Cousteau believes that the new ship should belong to all the people of the world. Instead of financing it through the large contributions from businesses or wealthy individuals, Cousteau wants to seek small contributions from hundreds of thousands of people all over the world. Each contributor would thereby own a small part of *Calypso II.*

It is an optimistic plan for financing a multimillion-dollar ship, but Cousteau is an optimist. Certainly, he is aware of the world's problems, but he does not believe that they cannot be solved. He intends to do his part—and he expects the rest of us to do ours.

Glossary

algae Simple types of plants with no true root, stem, or leaf, found in water.

anemia A weakened condition caused by a reduction in the number of red cells in the blood.

aqualung A type of self-contained underwater breathing apparatus invented by Jacques Cousteau and Émile Gagnan.

bathyscaphe A vessel for deep-sea exploration.

bathysphere A watertight observation chamber lowered by cables into the sea.

compressed air Air reduced in volume by being kept under pressure.

Conshelf The Continental Shelf Station, a manned underwater station.

coral reef A ridge made up of coral lying near the surface of the sea.

decompression sickness A condition caused by an excess of nitrogen forming bubbles in the blood; also called the bends.

diving bell A hollow, bell-shaped chamber in which a person can work underwater.

dry dock A place for repairing ships.

exhaust valve A device that lets used gases out of a tube or pipe.

hypothesis An unproved theory.

inert Inactive.

mine An underwater or underground explosive.

minesweeper A vessel designed to destroy mines.

mooring A place where a ship or underwater chamber is tied up.

nitrogen A heavy gas that makes up four-fifths of air.

nitrogen narcosis The inability to think clearly, caused by an excess of nitrogen in the body tissues.

oceanaut A person trained to live and work in an underwater environment; also called an aquanaut.

oceanography The study of the ocean environment.

oxygen A gas that makes up about one-fifth of air.

radiologist A person who works with X rays.

regulator The part of a breathing apparatus that controls the flow of gas.

salvage To save or rescue property, particularly from a wreck at sea; also the property saved.

screw propeller A device that moves a ship or plane, made up of two or more sheets of twisted metal.

SCUBA Self-contained underwater breathing apparatus.

Sea Spider A device for studying the surface layer of water.

snorkel A breathing tube that extends above the surface of the water.

strobe An electronically controlled mechanism that can give off short but intense flashes of light.

submersible An underwater vessel.

Turbosail™ A wind-powered sail used on a diesel-powered ship.

valve A device that regulates the flow of liquid or gas in a pipe.

zodiac A light, inflatable boat with an outboard motor.

Further Reading

Baines, John. *Protecting the Oceans.* Austin, TX: Raintree Steck-Vaughn, 1994.

Bright, Michael. *The Dying Sea.* Danbury, CT: Franklin Watts, 1992.

Conley, Andrea. *Window on the Deep: The Adventures of Underwater Explorer Sylvia Earle.* Danbury, CT: Franklin Watts, 1991.

Cousteau Society Staff. *An Adventure in the Amazon.* New York: Simon & Shuster, 1992.

Hackwell, W. John. *Diving to the Past: Recovering Ancient Wrecks.* New York: Macmillan, 1988.

Hirschi, Ron. *Save Our Oceans and Coasts.* New York: Bantam, 1993.

Humphrey, Kathryn L. *Shipwrecks: Terror and Treasure.* Danbury, CT: Franklin Watts, 1991.

Johnson, Rebecca L. *Diving into Darkness: A Submersible Explores the Sea.* Minneapolis, MN: Lerner, 1989.

Lambert, David. *Seas and Oceans.* Austin, TX: Raintree Steck-Vaughn, 1994.

Reef, Catherine. *Jacques Cousteau: Champion of the Sea.* New York: Twenty-First Century Books, 1992.

Rogers, Daniel. *Exploring the Sea.* New York: Franklin Watts, 1991.

Sinnott, Susan. *Jacques-Yves Cousteau: Undersea Adventurer.* Danbury, CT: Childrens Press, 1992.

Tesar, Jenny. *Threatened Oceans.* New York: Facts On File, 1992.

Waters, John F. *Deep-Sea Vents: Living Worlds Without the Sun.* New York: Dutton, 1994.

SOURCES

Cousteau, Jacques-Yves, with Dugan, James. *The Living Sea.* New York: Harper & Row, 1963.

Cousteau, J.Y., with Dumas, Frédéric. *The Silent World.* New York: Harper & Row, 1953.

Dugan, James, ed. *Jacques-Yves Cousteau's World Without Sun.* New York: Harper & Row, 1965.

Elandl, Bahgat, and Adel Rifat. *Interview with Cousteau.* *UNESCO Courier,* November 1991.

Transcript of David Frost interview with Cousteau, June 9, 1995.

Madsen, Axel. *Cousteau: An Unauthorized Biography.* New York: Beaufort Books, 1986.

Munson, Richard. *Cousteau: The Captain and His World.* New York: William Morrow and Company, 1989.

Tailliez, Philippe. *To Hidden Depths.* New York: E. P. Dutton & Company, 1954.

INDEX

Boldfaced, italicized page numbers include picture references.

Jacques Cousteau

Photo Credits
Cover (background): ©Leo de Wys, Inc./De Wys/Sipa/Grinberg; cover (inset) and pages 20–21, 34–35, 56, 58, 62, 64, 73, 74, 85, 90, 93, 100, 102, 105: AP/Wide World Photos; pages 4, 52, 83, 87, 88, 89, 91, 95: Photofest; pages 9, 13, 29, 43, 71: North Wind Picture Archives; page 66: J. Baylor Roberts/National Geographic Image Collection; pages 69, 77: Bates Littehales/National Geographic Image Collection; page 79: ©Rondi/Tani/ Photo Researchers, Inc.; page 81: Luis Marden/©National Geographic Society; page 98: ©Shirley/Richards/Photo Researchers, Inc.